ADVANCED SWIMMING

PHYSICAL
EDUCATION
ACTIVITIES
SERIES

Consulting Editor:
AILEENE LOCKHART
University of Southern California
Los Angeles, California

Evaluation Materials Editor:
JANE A. MOTT
Smith College
Northampton, Massachusetts

ARCHERY, Wayne C. McKinney
BADMINTON, Margaret Varner Bloss
BADMINTON, ADVANCED, Wynn Rogers
BASKETBALL FOR MEN, Glenn Wilkes
BASKETBALL FOR WOMEN, Frances Schaafsma
BIOPHYSICAL VALUES OF MUSCULAR ACTIVITY, E. C. Davis,
        Gene A. Logan, and Wayne C. McKinney
BOWLING, Joan Martin
CANOEING AND SAILING, Linda Vaughn and Richard Stratton
CIRCUIT TRAINING, Robert P. Sorani
CONDITIONING AND BASIC MOVEMENT CONCEPTS, Jane A. Mott
CONTEMPORARY SQUARE DANCE, Patricia A. Phillips
FENCING, Muriel Bower and Torao Mori
FIELD HOCKEY, Anne Delano
FIGURE SKATING, Marion Proctor
FOLK DANCE, Lois Ellfeldt
GOLF, Virginia L. Nance and E. C. Davis
GYMNASTICS FOR MEN, A. Bruce Frederick
GYMNASTICS FOR WOMEN, A. Bruce Frederick
HANDBALL, Michael Yessis
ICE HOCKEY, Don Hayes
JUDO, Daeshik Kim
KARATE AND PERSONAL DEFENSE, Daeshik Kim and Tom Leland
LACROSSE FOR GIRLS AND WOMEN, Anne Delano
MODERN DANCE, Esther E. Pease
PADDLEBALL, Philip E. Allsen and Alan Witbeck
PHYSICAL AND PHYSIOLOGICAL CONDITIONING FOR MEN, Benjamin Ricci
RUGBY, J. Gavin Reid
SKIING, Clayne Jensen and Karl Tucker
SKIN AND SCUBA DIVING, Albert A. Tillman
SOCCER, Richard L. Nelson
SOCCER AND SPEEDBALL FOR WOMEN, Jane A. Mott
SOCIAL DANCE, William F. Pillich
SOFTBALL, Marian E. Kneer and Charles L. McCord
SQUASH RACQUETS, Margaret Varner Bloss and Norman Bramall
SWIMMING, Betty J. Vickers and William J. Vincent
SWIMMING, ADVANCED, James A. Gaughran
TABLE TENNIS, Margaret Varner Bloss and J. R. Harrison
TAP DANCE, Barbara Nash
TENNIS, Joan Johnson and Paul Xanthos
TENNIS, ADVANCED, Chet Murphy
TRACK AND FIELD, Kenneth E. Foreman and Virginia L. Husted
TRAMPOLINING, Jeff T. Hennessy
VOLLEYBALL, Glen H. Egstrom and Frances Schaafsma
WEIGHT TRAINING, Philip J. Rasch
WRESTLING, Arnold Umbach and Warren R. Johnson

ADVANCED SWIMMING

JAMES A. GAUGHRAN
Stanford University

WM. C. BROWN COMPANY PUBLISHERS
Dubuque, Iowa

Copyright © 1972 by
Wm. C. Brown Company Publishers

Library of Congress Catalog Card Number: 72-81626

ISBN 0–697–07050–6

No TOC

Printed in the United States of America

Contents

CHAPTER   PAGE

Preface vii

1. What Advanced Swimming Is Like 1

2. Skills and Knowledge Essential for All
   Advanced Swimmers 4

3. Better Advanced Swimmers Achieve These
   Capabilities 26

4. Training for the Advanced Swimmer 37

5. Rules of Swimming 51

6. Unwritten Laws and Hints for Safety and
   Comfort in the Water 53

7. Language and Lore of Advanced Swimming 56

8. Where Do You Go from Here? 60

Selected References 62

Index 63

Preface

Once a swimmer has advanced beyond the "beginner" level and has developed his skills and swimming knowledge to the point where he can consider himself "advanced," he has before him a wide range of opportunities that he can take advantage of which are open only to the advanced swimmer. Not only are there suddenly within reach many exciting recreational and educational activities, both above and below water but the advanced swimmer can make great use of his ability to improve and maintain his health and physical condition. This book is designed to provide the swimmer who has gone beyond the beginner level with the technical know-how, swimming knowledge, and training techniques which he can utilize to develop himself into a truly advanced swimmer, and thus take advantage of those opportunities.

In addition to describing the most advanced techniques of modern day swimming, in Chapter 4 this book describes the up-to-date training methods used by today's top competitive swimmers and shows how to adapt those methods to fit the needs of the advanced swimmer at whatever stage of development he has attained. This book is therefore valuable not only to students and instructors in physical education swimming classes, but to all swimmers who have the desire to develop their swimming capabilities, improve their physical condition, and swim to a healthier life.

All swimmers, at all levels, will find herein a wealth of swimming information and helpful hints and cautions relating to all aspects of swimming, from stroke technique to swimming in the ocean. Gathered here are a wide variety of facts and aquatic knowledge, put together over a lifetime of coaching and teaching swimming at all levels, and presented in a way that will make your aquatic experience meaningful and rewarding.

Self-evaluation questions are distributed throughout these pages. They afford you typical examples of the kinds of understanding and levels of skill that you should be acquiring as you progress toward mastery of advanced swimming. You should not only answer the printed questions, but should pose additional ones as a self-check on learning. These evaluative materials are not necessarily positioned according to the presentation of given topics. In some instances you may find that you cannot respond fully and accurately to a question until you have read more extensively or have gained more experience. From time to time you should return to troublesome questions or to skill challenges until you are sure of the answers or have developed the skills called for, as the case may be.

What Advanced Swimming Is Like

1

Beyond the threshold of the intermediate swimmer lies a most exciting and diverse world that is closed off to the nonswimmer, who can it enter it only vicariously. While you are improving your skills and "watermanship" capabilities to the point of the advanced swimmer, you are not unlike Alice entering Wonderland, considering all the new, exciting, and challenging experiences and opportunities that await you. Not only will you have developed a pleasurable and very effective means of exercise, but you will have opened up the entire world of water-related activities, from skin and scuba diving, to water skiing, sailing, surfing, competitive swimming, water polo, and synchronized swimming, just to mention a few.

Who Is the Advanced Swimmer?

This book is written for the swimmer who has advanced beyond the "beginner" stage, and is ready for refinement of his basic skills and the development of advanced "watermanship" capabilities. To qualify as an *advanced swimmer* you should be able to perform the following swimming skills:

(1) Swim a minimum of 100 yards of each of the following basic strokes: sidestroke, breaststroke, crawl, back crawl, and elementary backstroke;
(2) Swim continuously for 400 yards, using any stroke or combination of strokes;
(3) Tread water for a minimum of 5 minutes;
(4) Maintain yourself afloat, with a minimum of movement for 10 minutes;
(5) Know and demonstrate the technique of "drownproofing";
(6) Be able to jump, and to do an adequate shallow dive from the side of the pool;
(7) Do a "pike" surface dive, and swim underwater for a minimum of 30 feet.

Basic learning progressions and drills to be used in acquiring the skills enumerated above are not within the scope of this book. Swimmers who have not yet reached that level of swimming achievement are advised to read *Swimming*, a book in this series (William C. Brown Company Publishers) by Betty J. Vickers and William J. Vincent, or other publications which devote particular attention to the learning of these basic swimming fundamentals, recommended for reading at the back of this book.

If you have developed skills and swimming endurance sufficiently to meet the above requirements, you are ready to enter into the world of swimming. You should now refine these skills, making certain that you are not only able to swim the strokes and perform the other swimming skills in a basic way, but that you are able to do so properly, utilizing the most efficient and modern techniques that have been developed. You are also ready to build swimming endurance to the point where swimming and all of its related activities can be enjoyed without your being unduly restricted by a lack of physical conditioning. As skills and endurance develop, you will find your in-the-water self-confidence soaring, as aquatic horizons open up before you. This book is written to provide you with the means to swim toward those horizons. The most efficient up-to-date stroke techniques and theories are presented for your consideration, as are the most modern training methods. Those training methods, easily adaptable to your physical conditioning needs, can be used to greatly improve your present distance and speed capabilities, at the same time improve your physical condition. Along with techniques and training methods, you will find a storehouse of swimming hints, facts, and cautions that will serve you well and add to your enjoyment of the sport.

Use of Your Advanced Swimming Skills

Physical Conditioning — The further we are removed from our frontier forefathers, and the more mechanized our society becomes, the more sedentary we become in our day-to-day lives. If we are to retain our health and vigor in the face of a way of life that makes little demand on us for physical exertion, we must develop our own programs for becoming and staying fit. The feeling of being in good physical condition can change the life of a person who has never before experienced it. Day to day activities no longer leave you feeling tired, and the spring in your step, combined with the solid feeling of a big breath of clean air, are enough to reward your efforts along the way.

One of the most efficient and enjoyable means of getting oneself in good physical condition, and staying there, is through swimming. It has truthfully been said that swimming exercises every muscle in your body, and it does so in a way that is the least likely to result in pulled muscles, bruised bones, or other ailments frequently associated with other physical conditioning methods. A training method which offers infinite variety, and which can be adapted to your abilities and stage of physical condition whether you are just beginning, or are a competitive swimmer, is presented in Chapter 4. This tremendous means to a healthier life is available only to you, the advanced swimmer. The giant bonus that awaits you as you extend your capabilities through training is the opportunity, again only open to you, to venture into the exciting world of water sports. All that, and a healthier life too.

Recreation — As leisure time and mobility increase each year, the range of available recreational opportunities increases as well. Everyone, to a greater or lesser degree, is within range of a pool, lake, river, or seashore, where abilities as an advanced swimmer can be taken advantage of to provide hours of pleasure. Sports such as sailing and water skiing become more enjoyable once one is comfortable and secure in the water. Just the fun of being able to confidently swim and play with family and friends in the water will justify the time you have spent. And, when the opportunity presents itself, because you are an advanced swimmer, you will be able to enter the exciting and beautiful realm of skin and scuba diving. These delights, and more, await you.

Water Safety — With your beginning skills, and particularly as you develop your techniques, endurance, and self-confidence, you will have become effectively safeguarded from the normal hazard of drowning. To be sure, unforeseen circumstances or misplaced judgement can still get you into trouble in the water, but you will be water-safe in ordinary situations. The next, and logical, step for you is to acquire the techniques and know-how of *lifesaving*. Not only will that learning experience further insulate you from drowning, but it will train you to properly handle other in-the-water emergencies that might arise in your presence. You will feel much more secure as your family or friends swim with you, knowing that you can help them if the need arises. It only takes a call to your local American Red Cross chapter to find out when the next Senior Life Saving course is to be offered. The few hours you will spend in earning your lifesaving card could be among the most valuable that you will ever spend for you and your family.

After you have earned your lifesaving card, it is time to consider an American Red Cross Water Safety Instructor's Course. This course will teach you how to teach the skills you have now acquired, both in swimming and lifesaving. Whether or not you plan to do any teaching, outside of your family or friends, this valuable experience is well worth your time.

In addition to the values of safeguarding and teaching those close to you, the fact that you hold a Red Cross Senior Lifesaving and/or Water Safety Instructor's card can be a valuable asset, particularly during your student years. Life-guarding and swimming instructor's jobs during the summer months are abundant, and they often pay very well. What more pleasurable way could there be to spend a summer than teaching small children to swim?

Competitive Aquatics — If you are so inclined, the abiltiy to swim well can open up the very diverse area of competitive equatics. Whether you prefer the individual competition of racing, the team aspect and rigors of water polo, or the grace and beauty of synchronized swimming or diving, there is something for you. Along with high school and college swimming, for both men and women, there is the vast A.A.U. age-group and senior program, and just gaining in popularity, senior age-group swimming, providing competition for adults right through the sixty-and-over age group.

2 Skills and Knowledge Essential for All Advanced Swimmers

In order to truly be an *advanced swimmer* you must develop and utilize proper techniques in the performance of the skills essential to advanced swimming. You must also build your working knowledge of the facts of "watermanship" that are essential to your full enjoyment, safety, and progress in the water. At this stage in your development as a swimmer, it is assumed that you have the basic abilities set forth in Chapter 1, which distinguish you from the beginning swimmer. It is now time to take a new look at the skills you have developed to make sure they are being performed in the most efficient and relaxed way possible, utilizing, where applicable, modern techniques which have been perfected in recent years. Particular attention will be paid to crawl stroke (commonly called "freestyle"), back crawl, elementary backstroke, breaststroke, sidestroke, underwater swimming, and butterfly. Most of these skills you have already developed to some extent. As an *advanced swimmer* it is essential that you now perfect your techniques so that you will be able to enjoy to the fullest the opportunities for fun, accomplishment, and physical development.

Relaxation — There are several basic principles of swimming which can be applied to many, if not all, the skills we are concerned with. Of primary importance in all swimming is *relaxation*. Just as relaxation is a key to learning beginning swimming skills, it is just as important now to the development of proper stroke technique.

Relaxation throughout the performance of all swimming skills results in the elimination of tense and jerky movements and enables you to direct all expended energies to the proper and efficient execution of the stroke or skill. Very little real effort or applied strength is needed for the execution of most swimming skills. It is only when real speed in swimming is involved that strength is important, and, even then, relaxation plays an important role in combination with properly applied strength. Tenseness in swimming is generally the result of a conscious or unconscious attempt by the swimmer to "hold himself up" in the water. As soon as this task is left to the swimmer's natural bouyancy, he can relax and concentrate on proper execution of the skill he is performing. This is of great importance to those who are not natural "floaters," but who can easily learn to stay on the surface with a minimum of relaxed movement.

Streamlining — Streamlining is another of the basic principles of swimming. The best illustration of the effect of streamlining on one's progress through the water is the action of a series of sticks thrown into a pool of water. A straight broomstick pushed through the water will move for some distance and in a straight line. A curved stick of the same length, weight, etc. will follow a path roughly approximating the curve of the stick, and, because of the friction of the water on the stick along the outer edge of the curve, it won't go as far as the straight stick. A stick with branches or bumps will not travel nearly as far as the straight stick. As elementary as the principle of streamlining is to swimming, it is often ignored by swimmers who consider themselves advanced, and they are consequently slowed down in their development. Streamlining begins with the push off the wall, or dive from the side. At the point of your pushoff or dive, you are moving at the fastest speed you will attain during your ensuing swim, and streamlining prolongs that speed. Streamlining for your dive or pushoff involves stretching your arms over your head, hands together, and pointing exactly in the direction of desired movement (the "straight stick"). Your head should be between your arms, with your ears touching your biceps, and not held up in order to look in the direction you are attempting to go. There must be no bend in your hips, and both your knees and ankles must be extended in the perfect *glide* position. (Figure 1.)

Figure 1—Streamlined glide position.

As you begin whatever stroke or skill you are performing, you should keep in mind the "straight stick" analogy—eliminating or minimizing any "branches" or "bumps" representing departures from that ideal. In keeping with proper streamlining then, stroke techniques that will present as streamlined a profile to the line of movement as possible should be used, such as the "whip kick" in breaststroke, as opposed to the wide knee recovery used in the more traditional breaststroke kick. The streamlining principle might be stated as a desire to present as little body area as possible in direct opposition to the direction of movement. It therefore follows that in the execution of all strokes and skills designed to move one through the water, one must, in addition to eliminating "branches," "bumps," and "curves" wherever possible, *maintain a position as close to the horizontal as possible.* This will minimize the drag, which increases in proportion to the angle your body assumes in the water. Your kick, therefore, in all strokes, should be done so as to keep your hips, legs, and feet close to the surface.

Stroke efficiency — Certainly if you are to swim any stroke with a minimum of effort and develop your distance and speed capabilities to their fullest, you must use stroke techniques that make the most of the amount of energy you expend. Relaxation and streamlining, as spelled out above, are basic ingredients in stroke efficiency, and to the extent that you incorporate them into your strokes, you will be eliminating a useless expenditure of energy. In addition to these characteristics of an efficient stroke it is required that you use stroke mechanics that most efficiently utilize the energy you are expending, so that you can swim a given distance at a given speed with the least amount of effort. A great deal can be learned about efficient stroke technique by examining the techniques and theories which have evolved in modern competitive swimming.

Arm Stroke

In order to move the greatest distance or go to the greatest speed possible for each arm stroke, you must use a technique that will apply force in the proper direction for the greatest length of time. The *amount* of force used, and thus the amount of energy expended, will depend on how much speed you want to develop. Whether you want to go fast, and expend your energy more quickly, or go at a slower pace for a greater distance, you should use a stroke that will enable you to do so most efficiently. The "bent-arm" technique, as applied to racing crawl, backstroke, butterfly, and breaststroke by today's top competitive coaches and their swimmers, can be fully utilized as you swim these, and other strokes that you have developed as an advanced swimmer. The inefficiencies involved in keeping the elbow extended through the power phase of the arm stroke, as opposed to gradually bending and then extending the arm through the power phase, are demonstrated in the illustrations contrasting the two techniques as they apply to the crawl and back-crawl strokes. (Figures 2 and 3.)

While the swimmer may actually expend as much or more energy in getting his arms through the water with the straight-arm technique, he will move a comparatively shorter distance and at a comparatively slower rate of

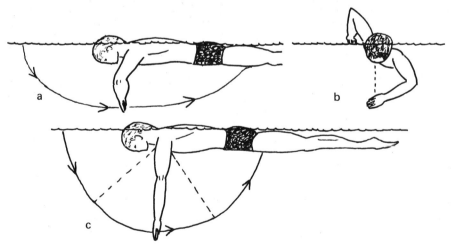

Figure 2—Crawl stroke arm pull. Contrasting power phase of bent-arm, (A), (B), and Straight-arm (C) styles.

speed than the swimmer using the bent-arm technique. The reason for this is clearly seen in figures 2 and 3, which show how relatively inefficient the various stages of the straight-arm stroke are in the application of force when compared with the corresponding stages of the bent-arm style. Even at that point in the stroke where the force is directed entirely opposite to the direction of movement (i.e., when the arm is directly under the shoulder), the straight-arm pull will not provide as much force as the bent-arm because of the inability of the swimmer to use his arm rotator muscles, which can come into play with the bent-arm technique.

A brief look at the arm pull used in each of the competitive strokes will demonstrate how the principle of the "bent arm" is applied in practice. You can put the principle to work yourself in swimming these and any other swimming strokes.

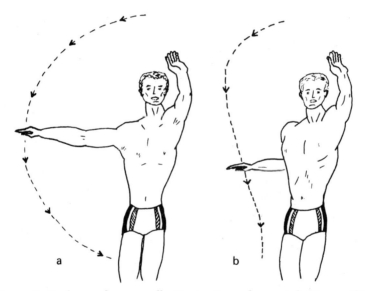

Figure 3—Back crawl arm pull. Contrasting phase of bent-arm, (B), and straight-arm, (A) styles.

Crawl stroke — Throughout the "recovery" stage of the crawl arm stroke, during which the swimmer's arm is brought forward in preparation for the power phase of the stroke, the elbow is held higher than the hand. This is particularly important during the final stage of the recovery, just prior to the hand entering the water in preparation for the "catch" and "pull" stages. As the hand enters the water in front of the swimmer's shoulder, the high elbow allows a smooth hand entry and brings the hand immediately into position for the catch as the swimmer begins to feel the pressure of the water on his hand, and literally catches hold of it in preparation for his pull. The catch may be delayed by stretching the arm and hand just under the surface of the water to effect a more gliding stroke. Once the catch is made on the

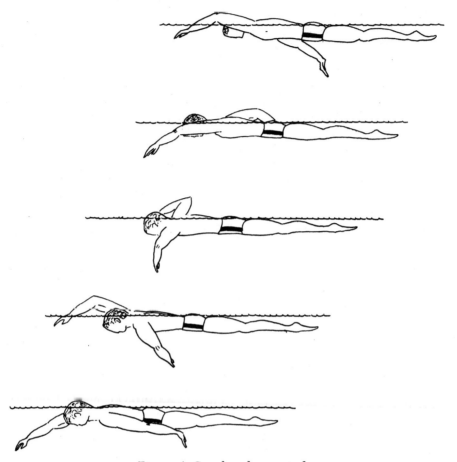

Figure 4—Crawl and arm stroke.

water, however, the pull should continue through until the "finish" of the stroke. As the catch is being made, and through the first part of the pull, the elbow must be kept higher than the hand. As the hand and forearm are drawn back along the line of pull, with the hand under the midline of the body, the arm is gradually bent, until at the midpoint in the stroke, when the arm is directly under the shoulder, it forms as sharp as a 90° angle at the elbow. From this point, the elbow, forearm, and hand continue to press backward into the final "push" phase of the stroke, as the arm is extended with the swimmer maintaining his hold on the water through the "finish," midway between his hip and knee. The finish, or last one-third of the power phase of the arm stroke, is accomplished largely through the action of the triceps extending the elbow. This portion of the stroke, emphasized in competitive swimming, is often forgotten by the beginner. Immediately, as the "finish" of the stroke is completed, the "recovery" begins with the hand clearing the water between the knee and hip as, with elbow high, the relaxed hand and

What are the two errors this crawl stroke swimmer is making?

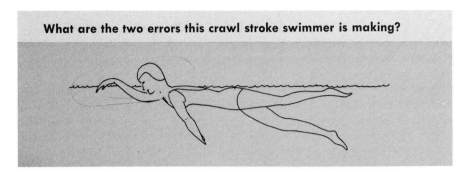

forearm are brought forward comfortably close to the body. The arm should not be swung around to the side in a straight-arm fashion, since the reaction to the wide swinging action will cause the body to sway out of its streamlined position. This stroke technique allows the efficient use of the driving force of the arm throughout the stroke, minimizing the inefficiencies that would otherwise come into play if you were to swim with the straight-arm style. (Figure 4.)

Back Crawl — The technique used in properly swimming the back crawl, or "racing backstroke," employs the same principle of the "bent arm" as described for the crawl stroke. The recovery of the arm is high and in line with the direction the swimmer is moving. As the hand enters the water over the swimmer's shoulder, the palm of the hand should be down, with the elbow fully extended. The hand immediately presses into the "catch" to a point about six to eight inches under the water where the pull begins. The elbow remains straight during the first quarter of the stroke, and then bends as the hand and forearm are brought down along the line of pull until again, at midpoint in the stroke the angle between the upper arm and forearm is as sharp as 90°. During the final half of the stroke, the arm is extended as the hand maintains its hold on the water through the finish of the stroke, ending with a final snap of the wrist, as though throwing the water being held down toward the swimmer's feet. The hand finishes just slightly to the side and below a point midway between the hip and knee. It is important in the execution of the arm pull for the back crawl that as your arm is bending through the first half of the stroke, you do not let your elbow bend in toward your body, but rather incline it toward the bottom of the pool, as illustrated. If done properly, your hand and elbow will both be at shoulder level at the midway point in the stroke. Once the elbow starts to lead the pull, it is like rowing a boat with a hinged paddle that folds up every time you pull through the water.

To perform your arm stroke most efficiently, you must rotate your shoulders and upper body sufficiently to enable you to perform the stroke comfortably, all the while keeping your head well back and motionless. Your upper body rotation must be along the line of direction you are moving so that you don't allow either your hips or shoulders to sway from side to side, destroying your streamlined body position. (Figure 5.)

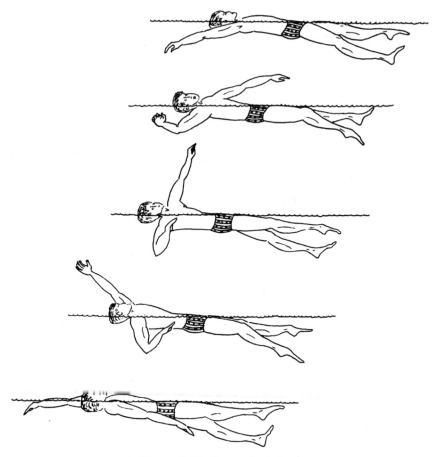

Figure 5—Back crawl stroke.

Butterfly — The arm pull used in the butterfly, in which both arms are recovered and pull simultaneously, is very similar to the pull described above for the crawl stroke. In the recovery phase, the arms are brought forward over the water, wide of the body, rotating the hands from the palms-up position that they are in at the finish of the stroke to a palms-(or at least thumbs-) down position at the point where the hands enter the water well ahead of the head, and generally from shoulder to head's width apart. At the point of entry, the elbow is held slightly above the hand to affect a smooth entry and to position the hand and arm for an immediate catch, as in the crawl stroke. The "pull," "push," and "finish" stages of the stroke are in general similar to the corresponding phases of the crawl stroke. Particular attention must be paid to the finish of the pull, at which point the hands must accelerate past the legs toward the outside as the recovery stage is entered into. (Figure 6.) There can be no hesitation between the finish and the recovery or you will get bogged down and be unable to bring your arms forward over the water.

Figure 6—Butterfly.

Figure 7—Improper body position during butterfly.

Here again proper streamlining is essential, and you must keep your hips and legs generally high in the water, so that the line of your body is in line with the direction you are swimming. As your hips and legs sink, you tend to go more up and down and less forward in the desired direction. (Figure 7.)

Breaststroke — The arm stroke used in swimming breaststroke as it has evolved in modern competitive swimming also incorporates the "bent-arm" style of swimming. The pull, as far as it goes, is very similar to that used in the first half of the crawl and butterfly. In the breaststroke, however, more emphasis is placed on the "glide" stage, during which the arms are both stretched forward. The glide is emphasized in the breaststroke in order to take advantage of the powerful thrust delivered by the breaststroke kick, which is not the case with crawl, back crawl, or butterfly. The arm pull should begin at any time from the point when the feet *finish the kick* until you feel yourself slowing down from the speed attained following the kick. If swimming for speed, the arm stroke will begin almost immediately as the kick finishes, but if speed is not your goal, you can glide from one to three

Figure 8—Breaststroke.

seconds before beginning the next pull. In swimming breaststroke on the surface, the arm pull should come back no farther than the shoulders due to the great amount of drag encountered as the arms are recovered underwater in preparation for the next stroke. As the catch is made and the pull started, the hands should press down and outward, moving slightly outside shoulder width. Keeping the elbows up, as in the first part of the crawl and butterfly pulls, the arms are brought back approximately along the line of movement until they are almost even with the shoulders. At that point, the hands are brought together under the chin and driven forward as the elbows are squeezed together for a streamlined extension forward. (Figure 8.)

All Strokes — The principles of the "bent-arm stroke," "catch," "pull," and "finish" can be applied to a greater or lesser degree to all swimming strokes, and by doing so you can make yourself much more efficient in their execution. Two additional swimming facts will help you to understand the effect of proper stroke mechanics. First, in strokes such as crawl, butterfly, and back crawl, an efficient swimmer's hand enters and leaves the water at very nearly the same point. It is almost as though you are able to reach out and pull yourself along through the water by grasping onto a series of handholds placed conveniently for you in the pool. This "solid" characteristic of water can easily be demonstrated by watching a good swimmer go by you and noting the exact point where his hand enters and leaves the water following his pull. The second swimming fact, related to the first, is that although water does in a way act almost as a solid substance which you can grab hold of to pull yourself along, you do begin to set in motion that part of the water directly behind your hand and forearm as you pull through your stroke. Therefore, if you are to get the full benefit from the "solid" property of water, it is necessary to either slightly change the path of your pull throughout the stroke in order to keep your hand in "still" water or accelerate your pull from beginning to end so that you continue to exert a positive force rather than letting your hand just move backward with the water you have set in motion.

Kicking

To the extent that the kick, in any stroke, exerts a force opposite to the direction of desired movement, it will assist you in making progress. Unfortunately for our swimming potential, our legs and feet are much better adapted for walking than for pushing us through the water. However, as you work on your kicking skills, keeping in mind the requirements for a good kick, this will help you in correcting mistakes you may be making and, in general, improve your kicking efficiency. Let's take a look at the four basic kicks—flutter, whip, dolphin, and scissors—to see what makes them go and to see how best to integrate them into our strokes.

The Flutter Kick — To see just what makes a flutter kick push one through the water, it is easier to first think of a swimmer using flipper fins. As he kicks along, the action of the flipper is easily observed as its long, flexible end bends back against the pressure of the water as the swimmer kicks down, so that the top of the flipper is, to a large extent, facing backward during the downward thrust of the kick, exerting force backward and pushing the swimmer forward. A similar effect is seen on the upward beat of the kick, with the bottom surface of the flipper now supplying the push. (Figure 9.)

In order, then, to derive any push from the flutter kick it will be necessary to have your feet imitate the action of the swim fins to some degree. This is not always easy, and some swimmers, whether beginners or competitive who have poor flexibility in their ankles find that they are able to make only very slow progress or none at all, while those who have great flexibility of the ankle, which allows more of the flipper-type action to take place, are able to move quite well using only the kick. Kicking in a slightly pigeon-toed manner will allow you to extend your ankle further, allowing more of the top surface of your foot to provide a backward thrust against the water as you kick downward. You can improve the flexibility of your ankles somewhat by doing stretching exercises. These exercises, which involve applying force to the top of the foot thereby hyperextending the ankle in order to extend the range of motion of the foot, are commonly done by competitive swimmers.

In the crawl stroke the kick is relatively inefficient in comparison with the arm stroke. That is to say, in order to go a given distance at a given speed, it takes a much greater expenditure of energy on the part of a swimmer using only his kick than it does to pull the distance using just his arms. In addition to its driving force, though, the kick does perform the very important function of keeping the legs and lower body up near the surface of the water to allow streamlined progress. The kick required to maintain good body position takes much less effort than that necessary to provide a driving force. Knowing these facts, it would be only sensible for you to minimize your kick when swimming long distances. Certainly if you find that because of a lack of ankle flexibility you are getting very little help from your kick, you should cut down the amount of energy you are putting into it, even on shorter swims, and use it primarily for maintenance of your body position. Indeed, many top competitive distance swimmers use only a one- or two-beat kick for each complete arm stroke, rather than the conventional six-beat kick of the "American" crawl employed by nearly all competitive swimmers for distances up to 200 yards. The economics of this are evident when you consider the size of the leg muscles and how hard they must work to get a comparatively small return from the kick, as compared to the much more efficient arm stroke. A swimmer in top shape can maintain a strong six beat kick over a 100- or 200-yard race, but a point of diminishing returns is reached soon after that. Many

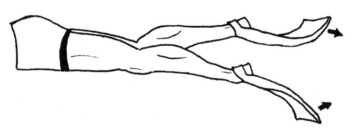

Figure 9—Propulsive action of swim fins.

swimmers do use a six-beat kick for even the longer swims, but it is considerably reduced in power. This is an important fact for you to remember as you set the pace of your training. Efficient expenditure of energy is one of the most important goals you should set for yourself as an advanced swimmer.

Much of what has been said about the flutter kick of the crawl stroke applies equally well to the back crawl. Because of the tendency of the legs to drop down, however, particularly if the head is carried too high or the hips dropped, it is usually necessary to maintain a steadier kick when performing that stroke in order to sustain your streamlined body position. Your knees should not come above the surface of the water during your kick while swimming the back crawl. To the extent that they do, it is an indication that you are using a "bicycle-riding"-type kick, which reduces the flipper-fin action needed to supply thrust.

The Whip Kick — The whip kick, as it has developed through competitive swimming, is much more efficient through its thrusting stage than the flutter kick and plays a relatively much greater role in moving the swimmer through the water. The kick in breaststroke is relied on to supply *at least* half of the moving force of the entire stroke. The source of this power can be seen in the side view of the whip kick shown in figure 8. After the feet are recovered, with both feet and knees remaining fairly close together, the feet are turned outward, presenting a large surface to catch and push the water backward through the finish of the kick. The relative position of the feet through the recovery and kicking stages is illustrated in figure 10. Several things play an important role in determining just how efficient the whip kick will be for you. First, the recovery stage of the kick must be done in a way to minimize the drag resulting when the knees and hip bend to bring the feet up into a position to begin their downward thrust. Keeping the knees no more than two to eight inches apart as the feet are drawn up is essential. It is particularly important during recovery not to let your knees drop too far down

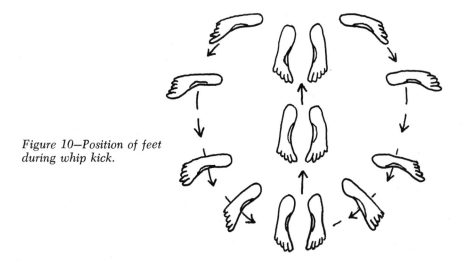

Figure 10—Position of feet during whip kick.

or be drawn up toward your stomach, since the resultant drag and loss of streamlining will tend to offset whatever positive effect you may get from the following kick. You might think of yourself during the recovery stage as a puppet with a string attached to the back of your heel, as opposed to your knee, so that when the string is pulled, your foot is brought up toward your seat along the surface of the water with a minimum dropping of the knee in the process. (Figure 11.)

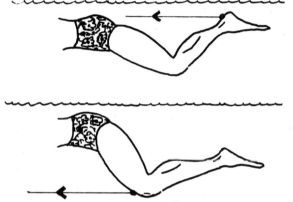

Figure 11—Proper (top) and improper (bottom) leg recovery for whip kick.

Once you have properly recovered your feet for the kick, you must turn them outward, with ankles flexed, to expose as much of the instep, side, and bottom of your feet as possible to the backward direction in order to provide a better catch and more powerful thrust as you drive your feet back and around to the finish of the kick. Note again the relative attitude of the feet throughout the kick, as illustrated in figure 10. It is important that as your feet whip around to the outside during the power phase of the kick, they stay wider than your knees. This lets the feet get out into "quieter" water for a more solid catch.

As with the flutter kick, flexibility will play an important role in determining just how well you can perform this kicking action and how efficient your kick will be. Immediately following recovery, you must rotate the bottom half of your legs to allow your feet to point outward, or to the sides, as indicated in figures 8 and 10. To the extent that you cannot do this and your feet remain pointed backward during the power phase, your kick will be correspondingly less effective.

At the finish of the kick, the feet complete the "whip" by snapping down, with ankles extending as the feet come together pointing backward in a streamlined glide position. The legs then remain fully extended through the first part of the arm pull, recovering in time to kick during the final stages of the arm recovery. The whip kick is not done on a "1-2-3" or "up-out-and-down" basis, as the older "frog" or "wedge" kick was done, but rather on a "1-2" or "up-and-around" basis. *The legs are never fully extended at the knee until the completion of the kick.*

Can you do the whip kick properly? Are you able to glide for 3 feet after each kick? 4 feet? 6 feet?

The Scissors Kick — The scissors kick, as used in the side stroke, is another very powerful kick when done properly. Its drawback, as with the whip kick, is the fact that the legs must be drawn up during recovery, and the resulting loss of streamline will all but stop you before you can begin the next powerful kick.

As with the whip kick, minimizing drag during the recovery stage is essential. Your feet and knees should be kept together as your legs are drawn up under your seat, much like the way you recover your legs for the whip kick. They are then extended forward and back, just under the surface of the water, with the forward leg fully extended, and the leg reaching backward flexed at the knee in preparation for the powerful thrust downward to the glide position (figure 12). Learn to do this kick on either side, and be able

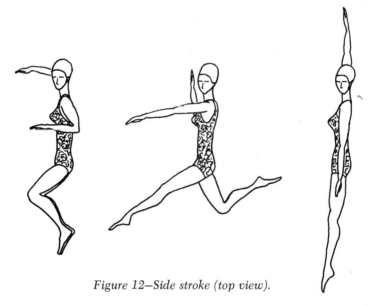

Figure 12—Side stroke (top view).

to do it with either the top or bottom leg extending forward. A top-leg-backward kick is preferred for use in lifesaving, whereas top-leg-forward is the most commonly used style for general swimming.

The Dolphin Kick — The principle use of the dolphin kick is in the butterfly stroke. As it utilizes the same up-and-down motion as the flutter kick, many of the same principles apply. Ankle flexibility is again of great importance in enabling the swimmer to employ more of the top surface of his foot in supplying a backward thrust.

In the dolphin kick, the powerful simultaneous downward thrust of the legs is initiated by a slight dropping of the knees, with the lower leg and feet following like the cracking of a whip. As the downward kick ends, the legs are fully extended and remain that way as they are recovered toward the surface of the water in preparation for the next downward kick. It is important not to recover the feet toward the surface by bending at the knees as you would when using the whip kick, since the resulting drag and loss of streamlining would greatly diminish the kick's effectiveness. (Figure 13.)

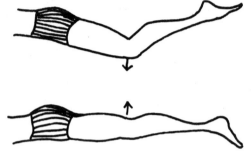

Figure 13—Leg action during dolphin kick and recovery.

With two kicks for each armstroke, the primary emphasis is put on the kick which comes during the final half of the power part of the armstroke, finishing just as the arm recovery begins. The second kick, usually of much less force and depth, comes just prior to the "catch" stage of the arm pull. It will help to coordinate the kick with the arms if you will lift your hips so that your seat comes above the level of the water just toward the end of the arm recovery as your hands are driving forward and down into the water. (Figure 6.)

Other Skills Essential to All Advanced Swimmers

Underwater Swimming – An advanced swimmer should be able to swim well underwater. The most effective stroke for underwater swimming is a full sweeping double arm pull utilizing the "bent-arm" technique as described for the crawl stroke, except that both arms are pulled through the stroke simultaneously. Following the pull, the arms are left extended backward along the legs during a gliding phase, before being recovered. As they are recovered, the hands should stay close to the body, being brought up along the stomach and chest to reduce drag; finally they are speared past your face to full extension in preparation for the next pull. Kicking preferences vary widely in underwater swimming; you can choose from any of the following: (a) the whip kick, which should be recovered at the same time as the arms, with the power phase coming just before the arm pull; (b) the flutter kick, which can be continued throughout the stroke; (c) the scissors kick, done with the timing of the whip kick; or (d) a combination of these. When swimming underwater with fins on, the most common and practical kick to use is a smooth, deep, flutter kick, giving the fins plenty of time to bend with the pressure of the water and provide their backward thrust. The dolphin kick is also sometimes used with fins.

Effects of Pressure — You have undoubtedly discovered some of the effects of pressure while swimming underwater. As you descend from the surface, the pressure exerted by the water on your body gradually increases at the rate of just under one-half pound per square inch for each foot of depth. Since the pressure exerted by the air on us at the surface is 14.7 pounds per square inch, the relative change in pressure is quite significant as you swim down from the surface. That pressure is exerted equally over your body, which, being essentially all solid and liquid, is incompressible and not noticeably affected, at least at normal free diving depths. What is effected, though, are the various air spaces in your body, including your lungs, sinuses, and middle ears. Your lungs and chest are quite elastic; so as you descend, the water pressure merely "squeezes" your chest and lungs, reducing your lung volume to the point where the pressure of the air in your lungs is equal to the pressure exerted from without, and you feel no difference even diving to twenty or thirty feet. Your sinuses are connected to your breathing passageways by small openings, and unless those are closed up, due to a cold, sinusitus, etc., the pressure in the sinus cavities will be equal to that of the air in the lungs and airways, which, due to the compression of the lungs, is the same as the surrounding outside pressure. When the sinus openings are clogged so that the "new" air pressure cannot be transmitted into the sinus cavities, however, a relative vacuum is formed, and the resulting negative pressure drawing on the tissues lining the sinuses causes pain. When this condition arises you should discontinue underwater swimming until the condition causing closure of your sinus openings is alleviated.

A similar situation exists with the ears. As you descend from the surface, the outside pressure pushes in on the ear drum, and unless the middle ear, which is an air cavity, can be brought up to an equal pressure, the stretching ear drum will begin to hurt and finally rupture should you continue your descent. This situation can, of course, be alleviated; "clearing the ears" is a routine matter for all skin and scuba divers. The middle ear is connected to the air passageways, by the eustachian tube. It is the equalizing of pressure through this tube that is the cause of your ears "popping" as you go up in the mountains or in an airplane. Unless this tube is closed because of the congestion of a cold or some other cause, you can transmit the pressure from your airways through the tube into your middle ear by holding your nose and gently blowing out, as though through your nose, while keeping your throat relaxed. That added pressure will force open the pliable eustachian tube, equalizing the pressure, and your ear drum will return to its normal state. As you continue to descend you must "clear" your ears every few feet as the surrounding pressure increases.

Because of the effect of increasing pressure as you descend in the water, you should avoid underwater swimming while using ear plugs. The pressure will tend to force them into your outer ear as a relative vacuum is created between your ear drum and the ear plug.

Hyperventilation — The dangers of hyperventilating in order to extend your underwater swimming should be well understood by the advanced swimmer. Hyperventilating results from taking several deep breaths in succession, usually as a means of extending breath-holding capacity. Breath can be held longer after hyperventilating. However, because of the risks involved, great caution should be exercised in its use, particularly in underwater swimming. Taking in and blowing out several large breaths in succession eliminates carbon dioxide from the air in the lungs, and to an extent the circulatory system. The carbon dioxide in the air we exhale is the by-product of our respiratory system. By taking several deep breaths in a row you can get ahead of your system, and, at least for a short while, have considerably less carbon dioxide in your system than would otherwise be the case. Since carbon dioxide building up in the circulatory system is the triggering device the body uses to communicate the need to take a breath, you will be able to go for a longer period of time without feeling the urge to breath. The problem with the whole procedure though is that in hyperventilating, while you can "blow off" the carbon dioxide, you are unable to add appreciably more oxygen to your system, and the oxygen in your last breath can be used up by your body before the carbon dioxide can build up enough to give you the urge to breath. What results is known as "shallow water blackout," a phenomenon in which the swimmer passes out from lack of oxygen without ever feeling the need to surface for a breath. Many good swimmers have drowned, even in shallow pools while using this method of extending their time underwater.

Surface Dives — An advanced swimmer should be able to do both a "pike" and "standing" surface dive to a depth of nine or ten feet without having to kick or take any arm strokes. The technique of the pike surface dive is generally well known to all advanced swimmers. Beginning from a face down position on the surface of the water, with both arms at your sides and palms facing down, pull your arms straight down until they are pointing at the bottom of the swimming area while bending from the waist so that your upper body and arms are pointing straight downward, with your legs remaining flat along the surface of the water. As your legs are then raised straight up into the air, this weight will push you down. You must be careful not to duck down too far or raise your legs so fast that they start to fall over, or you will end up diving at an angle to your objective. (Figure 14.)

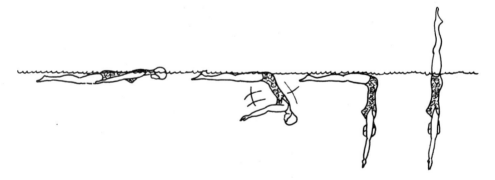

Figure 14—Pike surface dive.

Can you do a pike surface dive to 9 feet without arm strokes or kicks? a standing surface dive to 9 feet? to 12 feet with one arm stroke?

The standing surface dive, or "kelp dive," as it is known to skin and scuba divers, is begun in a standing position in the water. Simultaneously pushing downward with your arms and executing a scissors kick, lift yourself as far out of the water as possible. As you start to drop rapidly back into the water, turn the palms of your hands outward and begin a full sweep of the arms upward maintaining your "hold" on the water until your arms finally come together over your head. Your arms should not come out of the water during this maneuver. During the arm swing, be careful to keep legs straight and toes pointed downward so that you will go straight down, rather than off at an angle. This method of surface diving is commonly used by scuba divers to avoid tangling their scuba equipment in surface kelp, which would likely happen if the "pike" method were used. (Figure 15.)

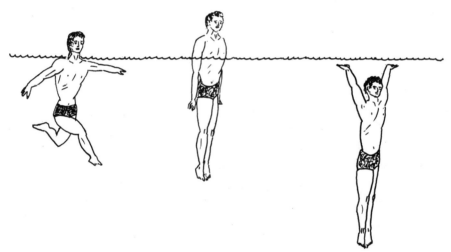

Figure 15—Standing surface dive.

Diving and Jumping

The advanced swimmer should be able to properly do a shallow and deep standing dive from the side of a pool, a feet-first jump and a front dive off a one-meter (or "low") springboard using a three- or four-step approach, and jump feet first from a height of ten feet.

When doing a standing dive from a stationary point, such as the side of a pool, there are several things that can be done in order to get good distance from the dive. First, be sure that your toes have a good hold of the front edge of your starting surface, since it is against that edge that you push to get your distance, not the top, flat surface. Next, as you push off, get your legs up higher than your hips (as illustrated in figure 16) so that you enter the water at an angle through an imaginary hole in the water. As your feet enter the water, raise your arms slightly so that they now point in the direction you want to go and parallel to the surface of the water, which will cause your extended legs to sweep down in an action very similar to the dolphin kick. The total effect will be to give you a comfortable dive with a maximum of distance.

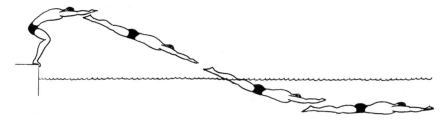

Figure 16—Front dive.

Springboard Diving — Once you can dive well from the side of a pool, the key to good springboard diving is the proper execution of the "approach," "hurdle," and "spring" preceding your dive from the board. Of primary importance is the requirement that you *never* run through the approach. From the starting point four or five normal steps from the end of the board (depending on whether you want to use a three-step-plus-hurdle or four-step-plus-hurdle approach), *walk* forward at a slow to normal rate, keeping your eyes on the end of the board. One step from the end, the hurdle is begun by pushing off with the foot taking the last step while lifting the opposite knee until the upper leg is parallel to the board. You must not lean either forward or backward during the approach or hurdle, so that as you come down with both feet an inch or two from the end of the board for your final spring upward, you are in a position to take full advantage of the board's springing action. To help maintain balance during the hurdle, raise your arms up in front of you, elbows extended, as you push upward into the hurdle, until they are fully extended over your head. As you come back to the board, your arms are brought down to the side, sweeping up and to the front again as you press upward and off the board. (Figure 17.)

Once in the air, you should come around easily at the top of your lift. Ducking your head down too early or too sharply will tend to throw your legs over your head. Enter the water fully extended with your head centered between your arms. It is a common error for a beginning diver to duck his head too far down just as he enters the water with the result that he smacks his head on the water rather than having it pass through the hole he has made in the surface with his hands. You must continue stretching toward the bot-

Can you do a forward approach and hurdle followed by a feet first entry into the water and stay within 6 feet of the board?

Figure 17—Springboard approach. Hurdle and takeoff.

tom, at least until after you feel your feet enter the water. Looking up or beginning to surface, too soon, while moving this fast through the water can cause great strain on the back. The danger of injury to the back increases, of course, in relation to the height from which you dive.

If you have difficulty in maintaining the position of your arms over your head as you enter the water, particularly when diving off heights greater than three feet, you might do what many competitive divers do—grasp the thumb of one hand in the fist of the other making a fist with each hand. Besides assuring you that your arms won't be wrenched apart by the force of the water while entering, this technique lets you "punch" a larger hole in the water through which your head can pass without smacking the water on the way.

When jumping feet first into water from heights greater than three feet, the main consideration is entering the water in a streamlined position. On leaving the board, platform, or whatever, you should keep your head upright and enter the water with your feet pointed down and arms at either your sides or over your head so as not to slap them on the water as you hit. The most common hazzard in jumping feet first, other than improper landings, is driving water up the nose and into the sinus cavities, which results in some discomfort and in possible sinusitis. This can be partially remedied by exhaling through the nose as you enter the water or by pushing the upper lip out to cover the nostrils just as you go in. Holding your nose is a good solution but may not be esthetically appealing to one who likes to think of himself as an advanced swimmer. Nose clips, if you can get them to work, will do the job too.

Push-Offs and Turns

One of the most common actions performed in swimming is pushing off from the pool wall. Whether pushing off following a turn or starting anew, if you use the proper technique and follow a couple of hints, you can get maximum distance. You will also save yourself considerable swimming if you are going a number of lengths of the pool.

Figures 18 and 19 illustrate one of the most basic requirements of a good push-off—that is, you should not push off from the wall until you have dropped under water to a point where your body is in line with the place on the wall on which your feet are pushing and until your body is facing the direction in which you want to go. Pushing off over the water without first dropping down will not give you maximum distance, since the weight of your body falling into the water pushes you too far down. In addition, with the force of your push being partly directed upward, you will not be able to drive off the wall as far as you would if the force of your push were directed entirely in the direction you want to go. The proper technique is easy enough when starting from a standing position (figure 18). When starting from the position shown in figure 19, however, whether starting anew or pushing off following an "open" turn (one in which you get a breath, as opposed to a racing "flip" turn), it is a very common error to push off as soon as the hand holding the wall lets go. The push-off should be delayed until that hand joins the other and the body is lined up properly underwater.

Streamlining is naturally quite important during the push-off. Because of your velocity, any misalignment will immediately throw you off course. Your head should be kept exactly aligned with your arms as you look down rather than in the direction of movement, or you will be slowed down considerably due to your resultant lack of streamlining.

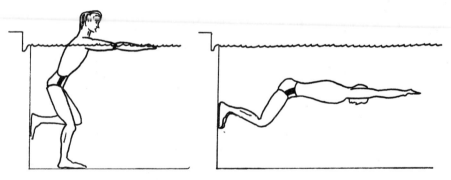

Figure 18—Standing push off.

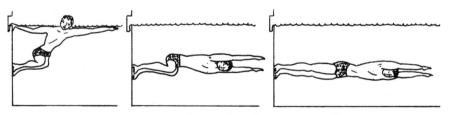

Figure 19—Push off when hanging on wall.

Backstroke open turns and push-offs follow the same principles and guidelines. In order to get good distance from the wall when pushing off on your back, you will have to keep your head back in a streamlined position. Since water will tend to go up your nose in that position, you should gently blow out air through your nose during your push-off and as you move away from the wall and toward the surface. (Fig. 20.)

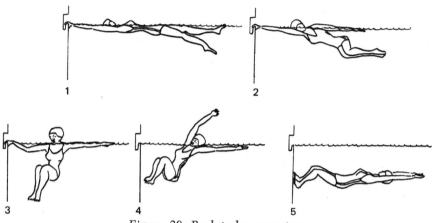

Figure 20—Backstroke open turn.

Open turns done while swimming on the stomach, side, or back can be speeded up by using the leading hand to push you around as you tuck your legs under your body. After pushing with the leading hand, let go of the gutter or pool railing as your legs swing under your body toward the wall, and bring your pushing arm over the water lining it up with your trailing arm just as your feet get to the wall for an immediate push. (See figure 20.)

As you push off from the wall, you should glide streamlined from fingers to toes for at least six to ten feet before starting first your kick, then your armstroke, as you continue swimming.

3 Better Advanced Swimmers Achieve These Capabilities

With the proper development of the skills outlined in Chapter 2, you are now ready to extend your capabilities and expand upon your knowledge and skills in all areas of swimming to the point where you can truly consider yourself a waterman.

Stroke Skills — When you are able to perform the basic skills outlined in Chapter 1, you will qualify as an advanced swimmer. However, until you are able to perform those skills easily and with good technique, you will not be comfortable in the water, and will not really be able to think of yourself as a waterman. The proper techniques for all the basic skills are outlined in Chapter 2; you must now apply yourself to the job of learning and mastering those techniques. The first "phase of training," set forth in Chapter 4, should be followed as you develop your basic stroke skills and prepare yourself to really enter into the world of the swimmer.

Swimming Endurance

To be confident as a swimmer you must, in addition to being able to perform the necessary skills well, develop your swimming endurance to the point where you can fully and comfortably enjoy the sport in its various recreational aspects and utilize it in improving and maintaining your physical condition. Reasonable goals for the truly advanced swimmer should include: (1) a continuous mile of swimming; (2) 400 yards of continuous swimming of each of the following strokes: crawl, breaststroke, sidestroke, backstroke (either elementary or back crawl); and (3) the ability to maintain yourself afloat treading water to float on your back, and to employ the technique of drownproofing, or any combination of these for an indefinite period of time. "Training Phase Two," in Chapter 4, is designed to assist you in extending your distance capabilities and in developing your overall endurance.

Swimming Speed

Swimming speed is important to the advanced swimmer only to the extent that speed is important in the particular aquatic activity in which he is participating. You can certainly be a good swimmer without being fast; most swimming activities can be fully enjoyed without regard to speed. There are, however, certain areas where some degree of swimming speed is an advantage. In lifesaving speed can certainly be an asset as it can in various water games, in racing, and in some aspects of surfacing and skin diving. Your own speed and how it improves is also one of the good gauges by which to measure your improving physical condition and technical skill improvement. One of the most highly developed arts in modern sports is the training of swimmers for the purpose of improving their swimming speed. "Training Phase Three," as set forth in Chapter 4, will give you quite a bit of insight into today's modern swimming training methods and how you can apply them to yourself.

The following table of swimming times is provided as a very general guideline to swimming performance for various distances and strokes and in order to give you a general idea of the goals you might set for yourself should you desire to develop your own swimming speed.

Table of Comparative Swimming Times

STROKE	DISTANCE	COMPETITIVE SWIMMING TIMES				NONCOMPETITIVE	
		BEST-M	AVER-M	BEST-W	AVER-W	GOOD	FAIR
CRAWL	25 yds	:10.3	:12	:12.5	:15	:16	:22
CRAWL	50 yds	:22	:25	:25.8	:30	:35	:45
CRAWL	100 yds	:47	:55	:56	1:05	1:10	1:30
CRAWL	200 yds	1:44	1:58	1:58	2:15	2:40	3:30
CRAWL	400 yds	3:44	4:10	4:05	5:00	6:00	8:00
CRAWL	1,650 yds	16:20	19:00	17:20	22:00	30:00	40:00
BACK CRAWL	100 yds	:54	1:03	1:02	1:13	1:25	1:45
BREAST	100 yds	1:01	1:12	1:10	1:21	1:35	1:55
BUTTERFLY	50 yds	:24.5	:29	:28	:37	:40	:50

The "best" times for men and women listed above are times under which the very best competitive swimmers perform. Thus, while the record for the 100-yard freestyle for men, for example, is under 45 seconds, swimmers capable of swimming faster than 47 seconds are among the very best. The "average" competitive times for men and women listed above are merely a general reflection of the times that a good beginning competitive swimmer might do at the college freshman or high school level. The "good" and "fair" noncompetitive times listed are for you to use as a guideline in setting your own time goals.

Starting Technique

Dive and Glide — As a better advanced swimmer, you should be able to dive from the side of a pool and glide for a good distance before starting to swim, and be able to push off from the pool wall and glide properly at the start of a swim or after a turn (see figures 18, 19 and 20). After a properly executed dive from the side (see figure 16), you should strive to glide for a minimum distance of fifteen feet before beginning to swim. Better swimmers diving in at the start of a swim are able to glide up to thirty feet before starting their kick and arm stroke, and in excess of forty feet when doing a "plunge for distance."

The Freestyle Racing Dive — The diving technique illustrated in figure 16, particularly as it shows the diver's position in the air and as he enters the water, is also an acceptable technique for racing. It is not necessary to land flat with a resounding smack as you hit the water in order to have a good racing dive. The angled entry shown in the illustration does have the desired effect of driving the swimmer forward as he raises his arms slightly at the moment his feet are entering the water, giving him a dolphin-type action of the legs. You must be careful not to go too deep, since in racing you want to be at the surface as soon as your glide slows down to your fastest swimming speed so that you can immediately start your stroke. Just after your feet enter the water on a racing dive, you should begin kicking in order to maintain your speed and to drive you toward the surface.

Figure 21 (a) illustrates the conventional starting position for the racing dive. Assuming the starting position, you should put your weight slightly forward on the balls of your feet but keep your heels in contact with the starting block while retaining your balance. At the signal to go, you must begin your armswing up and backward while dropping your knees slightly as you prepare to drive off the front surface of the starting block (figure 21[b]). As your arms complete their circle and add weight to your outward momentum, you should drive off the block at an angle slightly upward to get the maximum distance possible before entering the water. Note that at no time during the start do you rise up any higher than your original position. (Figure 21.)

Figure 21—Conventional racing start.

Figure 22 illustrates a recently accepted starting technique often used in competitive swimming today known as the "grab start." At the command to take your mark, the swimmer comes down to a position where he can grab the front edge of the starting block just outside his feet. By doing this he can lean a bit further forward before the start. On the signal to go, he should push against the starting block with his hands. This will have the effect of getting him off the blocks faster than by using the more conventional start. Following his push against the edge of the block with his hands, he should then drive his arms straight forward and attempt to drive out from the block as far as he

This swimmer is pushing off the wall following a crawl stroke "open" turn. What error is she making?

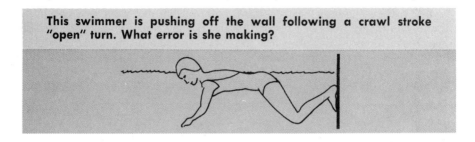

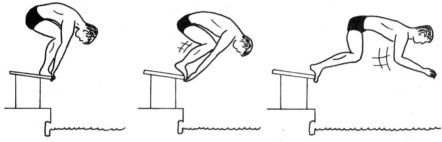

Figure 22—The grab start.

can. The possible drawback to this dive is that although the swimmer gets off the block first, he is generally not able to get out as far as the swimmer using the conventional start because of his initial low starting position and lack of armswing momentum. (Figure 22.)

Racing Turns

Racing turns are useful mainly for competitive purposes and thus are not a mandatory skill for the advanced swimmer. The "flip-turn" is a handy turning technique though when you do find yourself in a race, or to use in your speed training. The flip-turn is done under water so you don't get a breath on the turn as you would with an "open" turn. However, that luxury is universally dispensed with by top competitive freestylers in the interest of speed, even in races as long as 1,650 yards (or 1,500 meters).

The Front Flip-Turn — The front flip-turn, used in crawl stroke (freestyle) racing, can be simply described as a forward somersault with a one-quarter twist added, so that the swimmer ends up on his side rather than on his back at the completion of the flip. There are several variations of the flip-turn, the most common being illustrated in figure 23. In performing the flip-turn, you must be careful to bring your hand quickly around so as not to end up to deep in the water. It is important when doing this turn that you keep yourself properly oriented so that you can push off the wall immediately and with confidence that you will be headed back in the proper line of direction. As you go through your turn, it will be helpful if you can keep a point on the bottom of the pool in sight. Note that in figure 23 the swimmer coming in with his right hand leading as he starts his turn is able to watch the lane-end marking on the adjacent lane to his right throughout the turn. The result will be that by keeping your head facing slightly in that direction, you will bring about the one-quarter twist needed to end up on your side, and you will be completely oriented as you finish the flip. Your hands and arms should be fully extended over your head by the time your feet get to the wall so that you can immediately push off. (Figure 23.)

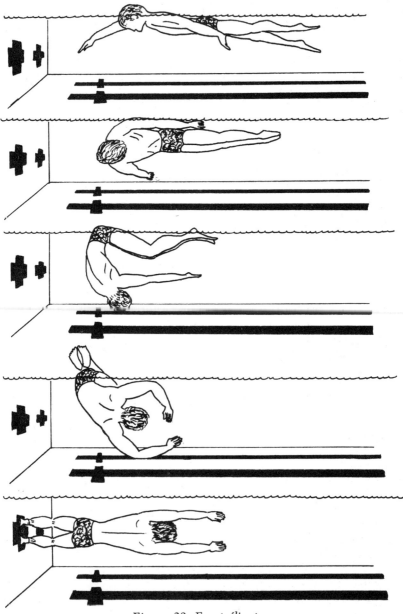

Figure 23—Front flip turn.

The Back Flip-Turn — The back flip-turn is not really a flip at all but more of a spin-turn. Use your upper back as a pivot as your legs are brought around over the water. Here again, being aware of your directions as you execute the turn is quite important to insure a straight push-off. After your legs are more than half way to the wall, you will be able to see the place on the wall when your hand has been pushing. You can watch that point until just before your legs are ready to push off, and, at that point, you must drop your head back into a streamlined position for the push-off. (Figure 24.)

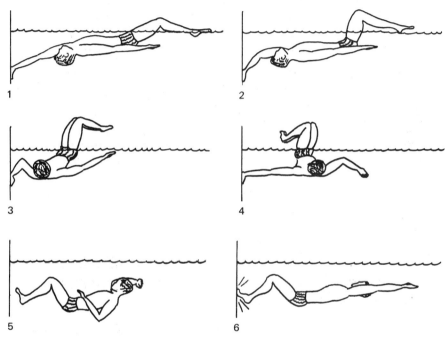

Figure 24—Back flip turn.

Life Saving Skills

As an advanced swimmer and one who will consequently be spending considerable time around the water, it is vital that you have at least basic lifesaving skills. If at all possible, you should take advantage of the American Red Cross lifesaving courses that are offered through your local Red Cross chapter or, at the very least, familiarize yourself with the available Red Cross lifesaving literature.

The basic rule of lifesaving is to go into the water to make a rescue *only as a last resort.* You should familiarize yourself with the use of "reaching assists," such as poles, ropes, boards, etc. in helping the person needing assistance to reach the side of the swimming area. It takes a strong swimmer who knows what he is about, to go into deep water to rescue someone on a one-on-one basis. If you use your head, you can usually find an available alternative.

All swimmers should know and practice the procedures and techniques for mouth-to-mouth resuscitation, the easiest and most effective method of artificial respiration. The steps to be followed in administering this method of resuscitation, also known as "rescue breathing," are as follows:

(1) Clear any foreign matter out of the victim's mouth with your fingers.

(2) Tilt the victim's head back so that his chin points upward, thereby opening up the air passageway. You may have to grab hold of the jaw with your thumb in the victim's mouth to pull his jaw outward if his tongue is still back against his throat blocking the free passage of air.

(3) Pinch the victim's nose closed with your free hand, and, placing your mouth tightly over the victim's mouth, blow air into his lungs. If the air passageway is open, you will be able to see his chest rise as you blow. If it appears that you are not getting adequate air into the victim's lungs, recheck his mouth for obstructions and be sure his head is well back and his jaw forward.

(4) Allow the air to escape by removing your mouth. There is no need to push the air out by pressing on the victim's chest. The elasticity of the chest and lungs will take care of that.

(5) Repeat the blowing effort and continue at a rate of about twelve breaths per minute for adults, and up to as many as twenty shallower breaths per minute for small children.

Resuscitation should be begun immediately upon recovery of the victim. Often this method can be initiated while the victim is still in the water. You must be careful in performing mouth-to-mouth resuscitation not to overbreath yourself to the point of dizziness. If prolonged resuscitation is required, it is best to trade off with a partner every two or three minutes. Artificial respiration should be continued until the victim begins to breathe for himself, he is pronounced dead by a physician, or no doubt remains that he can't be revived.

Advanced Springboard Diving

Springboard diving is an activity requiring skills and physical attributes in addition to those called for in advanced swimming. Good diving at the advanced level, in addition to requiring coordination, also calls for balance and considerable gymnastic ability, particularly in the execution of somersaults and twisting dives common to competitive diving. As an advanced swimmer, the ability to properly do both a controlled front dive and a feet-first jump following a well executed three- or four-step approach (see figure 17) will give you a good entree into this specialized field.

Skin Diving Skills

After you have developed your advanced swimming skills to the point where you are comfortable in the water and have confidence in your general abilities, one of the most enjoyable and exciting applications to which you can put those skills is the field of skin and scuba diving. As you have been developing your swimming strokes, endurance, underwater ability, surface dives, etc., you have been providing yourself with all the tools necessary to qualify you for instruction as a skin and scuba diver.

Skin diving, also known as "free diving," (as opposed to "scuba diving"), refers to surface and underwater swimming where a face plate and usually fins and a snorkle are used. Scuba diving refers to underwater swimming while breathing by means of a *self-contained underwater breathing apparatus* (the first letters combining to spell "scuba"). In order to purchase scuba gear or have your scuba tank charged with air, reputable dealers usually require evidence that you have been properly certified by a recognized certifying agency. To be certified you must take a scuba diving course generally entailing a minimum of thirty hours of instruction.

Instruction in skin diving is also available and would certainly be an advisable introduction to the sport. You can fully enjoy this inexpensive and fascinating pastime, however, by utilizing your advanced swimming skills and by learning some basic skin diving rules and facts. The basic equipment of the skin diver includes the face plate (or mask), which encloses his nose and eyes in order to allow equalization of the pressure inside the mask (which the diver can do by exhaling slightly through his nose as he descends in the water), swim fins, and a snorkle to breath through as he moves along the surface, face down, watching the underwater action. A couple of hints regarding skin diving equipment should be considered when buying the basic items. (1) Your mask should be made with safety, or tempered, glass, *not plastic*. Plastic will repeatedly fog over while you are diving. This can be prevented with glass by rubbing saliva around on the inside of the glass and rinsing it out prior to diving. (2) Your fins should not be too big, or the action of your foot in the loose fin will immediately raise blisters. (3) Your snorkle should be of the simple "J" variety, of adequate diameter to allow easy breathing, and should have a mouthpiece that will not close off as you bite down.

In skin diving, as in all swimming, the "buddy system" is the only way to go. Since in skin diving you will be repeatedly diving to depths below six feet, you should review the procedure for clearing your ears so that you can easily equalize the pressure in your middle ear to that of the surrounding water as you descend thereby avoiding the pain that will otherwise occur as the outside pressure increases. While diving, you will be striving to extend your breath-holding capabilities, and as you do so, you must be aware of the dangers of hyperventilation. Both "ear clearing" and hyperventilation are extensively discussed in Chapter 2. For additional information on skin and scuba diving, see "Selected References" following Chapter 8.

As a better advanced swimmer and in preparation for your future in skin and scuba diving, you should develop your underwater capabilities to the point where you can dive from the surface to a depth of fifteen feet or more, clearing your ears progressively as you go, and swim a distance of at least sixty feet underwater without the use of fins.

Ocean Swimming

Much skin diving and recreational swimming will be in ocean waters (if you are fortunate enough to live near a seashore), and while the ocean provides a wonderful environment in which to swim, you must approach it with a great deal of respect and caution. The basic caution for all swimming, that you *know your limitations*, applies with particular force when swimming in the ocean. Again, swimming with a buddy is only common sense. You should always fully acquaint yourself with the existing situations and conditions and evaluate them in the light of your limitations before entering the water. Among the things you should consider are the following: (1) the temperature of the water; (2) the depth of the water and rate of drop off; (3) the size of the waves and your ability to handle them; (4) the existence of an undertow; (5) the existence of riptides or other currents; (6) the presence of stinging jellyfish in the area; (7) the presence of sea urchins, sting rays, or other marine organisms in shallow water which you might step on while wading; (8) the location of the lifeguard in case of an emergency. These conditions and situations are not merely items for the beginner to worry about. Every top ocean swimmer will consciously or unconsciously check off in his mind each of these considerations as he prepares to enter the water.

Riptides and Undertows — A riptide results when water thrown up on the shore by wave action forms a channel as it returns to the sea. When it is fed by water of succeeding waves, it becomes a current moving away from the beach. "Rips" are generally not very wide, maybe twenty to sixty feet depending on the size and amount of wave action, and they will disperse generally twenty-five to fifty yards offshore. If caught in a riptide, you should swim as though going parallel to shore rather than trying to fight it by swimming directly toward shore against the action of the rip current. As you finally swim across and out of the rip or drift out with it until it disperses, you can then return to the beach, making sure you stay wide of the current. As you stand on a beach, particularly if you can get a high vantage point, you can generally spot a riptide. The water moving away from the beach making up the tip will look darker or dirtier because of the sand it has picked up. The action of the rip also tends to diminish the wave action in its path. (Figure 25.)

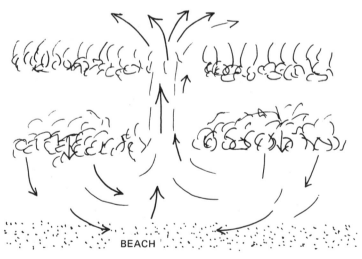

Figure 25—Rip tide caused by wave action.

An undertow is the result of water which has been thrown up on a steep beach by wave action returning to sea and passing under any immediately following waves or surface water. The undertow disperses very rapidly and not far from shore due to the relatively small amount of water involved. It is dangerous, however, to the wader or tired swimmer, whose feet may be swept out from under him just as the next wave arrives. (Figure 26.)

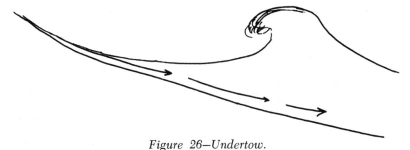

Figure 26—Undertow.

Body Surfing — Body surfing is the art of riding the waves without the aid of a flotation or planing devise, such as a surf board, surf mat, or belly board. Because of the lack of equipment, (although swim fins are recommended) the opportunity to use swimming skills, and the intimate relationship the swimmer has with the water, body surfing is one of the most enjoyable of ocean pastimes. Starting in small waves close to shore and using the bottom to push from just as the wave reaches you, you can learn to surf in with the wave: first with arms held in front as though pushing off from a wall to start swimming and then bringing one or both arms to your sides and pressing them, elbows extended and palms up, slightly down below your legs to act in the manner of hydrofoils, allowing you to then raise your head as you ride toward shore. Being able to "catch" and stay with a wave when body surfing is a result of sliding down the front of the wave. You must, therefore, keep your feet and legs higher than your head, or the wave will go by you. After learning to surf straight ahead and to get your head up while moving toward shore, you should learn to ride across the wave in order to be moving parallel to the shore as you go in on the wave. The ideal surfing action is to travel sideways and down a wave keeping just ahead of the breaking portion so that you have a smooth, fast ride toward shore. (Figure 27.)

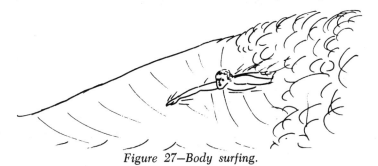

Figure 27—Body surfing.

Diving Under Incoming Waves — An essential skill requisite to body surfing is the ability to properly take care of yourself while swimming in water where waves are approaching and often breaking in front or on top of you as you wait for a proper wave to ride, or when you are moving out through the surf line after riding a wave toward shore. As you learn by experience and get to know the wave action on a particular beach, you can jump or float up over incoming swells before they start to break. Waves are sometimes deceptive, though, and wave action varies from beach to beach depending on many variables. Until you are sure of what you are doing, you should dive under swells that are bigger than you can easily stand off. Waves that have broken before they reach you or that are about to break on top of you must be treated with respect, since there is plenty of power in that fast moving water. You should dive under these waves. You should begin your dive when the wave gets within six to twelve feet from you (depending on the size of the wave) and angle down toward the bottom at about a 45° angle, staying down until you feel the wave pass over you. You should then surface and immediately look in the direction of the incoming swells to see if you have to prepare to make another dive. This method is not difficult, even in large surf. It does require, however, that you be in excellent condition, since repeatedly diving under waves in which you get caught with a big set of waves rolling in is very tiring. You must know and honor your limitations when deciding to go out into surf of any size. (Figure 28.)

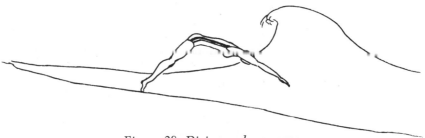

Figure 28—Diving under a wave.

Are You A Waterman?

As an advanced swimmer, the combination of advanced skills and aquatic know-how set forth in this chapter are certainly within your reach. When you are able to master those skills and build your own "aquatic sense" through personal observation and experience, you will be able to fully enjoy and take advantage of the unlimited opportunities available to you through swimming. As your self-assurance and confidence are built and supported by your accomplishments, you will begin to realize that you are indeed a waterman. That is a very worthwhile goal and a satisfying accomplishment for any man or woman.

Training for
the Advanced Swimmer

4

In order to fully take advantage of your present abilities as an advanced swimmer and to extend your capabilities you must put yourself into a training program specifically designed to assist you in achieving your goals along the way. Your overall goals in training should be: (1) to perfect your swimming skills by developing proper stroke technique; (2) to extend your present swimming capabilities; and (3) to improve your overall physical condition. These goals are all, of course, interrelated, and improvement in one area will result in some improvement in the others. However, your training program should be designed to allow consideration on one area at a time in order to achieve maximum results in each.

We will, therefore, separate training into the following three phases:

(1) A stroke improvemnt phase in which you should work on developing proper technique in all your basic strokes;

(2) A phase devoted to the extension of your distance capabilities;

(3) A phase devoted to improving the speed of your swimming and your overall physical condition.

Personal goals can and should be set in each of these phases of training. A personal log (or diary) should be kept so that you will be able to keep track of your progress. As you move from one phase of training to the next, the various criteria presented for you to use in judging your progress will allow an endless variety in the training program. There will always be room to improve, and as you achieve early goals, new ones should be set based on your newly developed capabilities. The fun and continual sense of accomplishment that will be yours is very real, since in training you will see remarkable self-progress as you gauge your performance against your past records, attain your goals, and reset them again and again. With the continual improvement you make in these areas, you simultaneously increase self-reliance and confidence as an advanced swimmer and will be well on your way to becoming a waterman.

The Interval Training Method

Almost without exception, all swimming training for competitive swimmers today is done under the "interval training method." It is largely this

Can you swim four times 50 yards with 30 seconds rest between 50's and hold a steady pace? Can you hold the same pace swimming two times 100 yards with 1 minute rest between 100's?

training method, as administered and extended by today's competitive coaches, that has been responsible for the dramatic and repetitive toppling of all swimming records, particularly since the mid-1950s. In essence, interval training calls for the swimmer to swim, kick (legs only), or pull (arms only) a given distance (e.g., 100 yards), a given number of times (e.g., 10 × 100 yards), at a given rate of speed (e.g., 60 seconds for each 100-yard effort), with a great rest interval between each of the repeated efforts (e.g., a 30-second rest between each of the ten 100-yard swims). Since a coach can alter each of the variables inherent in the system (i.e., stroke to be used; whether the series of efforts is to be swum, kicked, or pulled; the distance to be repeated; the number of repeats; the speed; and the rest interval) he can devise workouts of infinite variety and with changing emphasis, depending on his plan for any particular stage of the season. Although in the past coaches did introduce repetitive efforts at a given distance into their training programs or workouts, it was never done to an extent even approximating today's widespread and intensively applied interval training methods.

Today's training can be contrasted with older methods which put primary emphasis on continual swimming. For instance, under earlier training methods, a swimmer might have been told to swim 1,000 yards at as good a pace as he could maintain, regardless of the fact that his racing distance was 100 or 200 yards. He would typically do that 1,000 yards today by swimming a series of shorter-distance efforts (e.g., 5 × 200 yards, 10 × 100 yards, or 20 × 50 yards) with short-interval rests between each repeat effort, and he would swim each segment at a speed much closer to his racing pace than would be possible if he were to swim the 1,000 straight. This method allows a much greater extension of the swimmer's cardiovascular capabilities than the former method, if the swimmer applies himself. He is allowed to train in a way that has a much greater relation to actual competitive conditions insofar as the stroke technique he is using, his body position in the water, and the effort he is putting forth.

A complete workout under former training methods might have called for the swimmer to pull 1,000 yards, kick 1,000 yards, and swim 1,000 yards. That workout (totaling 3,000 yards) could be done with much greater training effect, as follows: Pull 10 × 100 yards, taking a 20-second rest between 100s; Kick 5 × 200 yards, taking a 1-minute rest between 200s; Swim 6 × 100 yards, starting every 2 minutes; Swim 2 sets of 4 × 50 yards, taking a 10-second rest between 50s, and a 2-minute rest between each set of four 50s. The swimmer should go each set of repeat efforts as hard as he feels he can go, given the distance, number of repeats in the series, and the amount of the rest interval.

In addition to the increase in the intensity of work done because of the adoption of the interval training method, competitive swimmers today are swimming a much greater total distance in daily training than in the past.

The distance a typical competitive swimmer swims daily in a strong program has increased over the past twenty years from between 1,500 and 3,000 yards, to between 7,000 and 14,000 yards. This fact, combined with the intensity of training today and a full-blown age-group swimming program, has resulted in current swimming performances that were thought impossible just a few years ago.

Keeping in mind, then, training methods which are being so successfully applied to competitive swimming today, you can formulate your own training program by utilizing modern training methods (scaled down, of course) so that you, as an advanced swimmer, can achieve your personal goals, just as the competitive swimmer does at a different level of performance.

Sample workouts are given for each of the successive phases of your training program. They are to be used as examples of the type of work you should be doing at a particular stage of your training and as guidelines while moving from one phase of training to the next. By knowing the variables to be worked with under the interval training method, you can devise your own workouts and keep them interesting and varied as you assume the role of your own coach.

Warming Up — In all phases of your training program you should precede your workout with a period of warming up. The purpose of the warm-up is to get your body ready for the coming effort so that you don't catch it by surprise before it is ready to take on the task you've set for it. You want to "wake" up your circulation system so that adequate oxygen can be delivered to your muscles as they take on the work of swimming. Without a proper warm-up, it is likely that you will experience a sudden feeling of fatigue shortly after you begin, even though you are operating well within your normal capabilities. You then have to wait while your body catches up with your impulsive start and until you catch your "second wind." Therefore, before you get into your planned workout, a series of swims, kicks, and pulls, at an easy pace will leave you better prepared to pursue your goals for the workout.

What Stroke To Use — As you move from one phase of training to the next, you should continue to utilize all of your basic strokes to a greater or lesser extent. Not only will you then continue to improve your technique in those strokes and insure your overall physical development (since some strokes use muscles not used in others), but as you set stroke, distance, and speed goals for yourself in each stroke you will provide a great deal of variety for your workouts. This is particularly important, of course, in the first phase of your training where you will be perfecting your stroke techniques. As you move on to where the primary interest is improvement of your physical condition, you will find that the best training effect will be realized by utilizing strokes calling for a more continuous effort, such as crawl, back crawl, and butterfly, than by using the gliding- or resting-type strokes, such as breaststroke, elementary backstroke, and sidestroke.

Where To Begin — You may now be wondering just how and where to begin your training and whether or not you have to go through the training phases in order rather than jumping right into speed or physical conditioning training. Although the swimming done in each phase of training will naturally result in progress that will carry over to the succeeding phases, you should begin your training program by concentrating first on Phase One until you have properly developed your stroke, and then, Phase Two, as you extend your distance capabilities. Emphasis can later be shifted to speed and conditioning after a solid basis for such work has been established.

Phase One — Developing Proper Stroke Technique

Your first phase of training is not a strenuous one since there will be no emphasis on speed or distance. It is, however, a vitally important stage in your training in that it forms the basis for all of the swimming that is to follow. While you certainly don't have to develop all of your strokes to perfection at once, you should be sure that before setting distance or speed goals in a particular stroke, you are able to swim it with proper technique and efficiency, At this stage you should be continually working on relaxation and streamlining in addition to stroke mechanics. You should pay particular attention to the principles set forth in Chapter Two and apply them to your swimming. You must also take advantage of whatever additional correctional tools are available to you, including swimming instructors, movies of yourself swimming, etc. It is much to your advantage to correct and properly develop your stroke at this stage rather than to go right into longer repetitive training, which has as its goal the development of other capabilities and would only tend to "groove in" whatever mistakes you may currently be making in your stroke.

You should therefore seek out whatever help is available to you and develop your techniques first by swimming shorter distances under instruction, so that you can develop your stroke while you are not tired, which would only tend to distort your efforts. Swimming a repeated distance of from 20 to 100 yards with an adequate rest interval taken between swims to fully recover and absorb the criticism of your instructor is certainly sufficient and much more to your purpose at this stage than longer or more repetitive swims.

One yardstick by which you can sometimes gauge your early progress is the number of strokes taken to swim a given distance. As you swim at a relaxed pace, the more efficient your stroke and the more relaxed and streamlined you become, the fewer strokes it will take you to go a given distance. This test is a good indicator of your progress and stroke efficiency because you can easily apply it to yourself to check your progress in an area where it is otherwise difficult to measure improvement without the help of an instructor. Stroke count is not a very precise gauge, since other factors not re-

GUIDE TO YOUR STROKE COUNT EFFICIENCY—25 YARDS FOLLOWING PUSH-OFF

STROKE USED	OUTSTANDING	VERY GOOD	GOOD	FAIR
Crawl	12-15	16-19	20-25	26-30
Back Crawl	14-17	18-21	22-27	28-32
Breaststroke	7-9	10-12	13-15	16-18
Sidestroke	8-10	11-13	14-16	17-19
Elementary Backstroke	7-9	10-12	13-15	16-18
Butterfly	8-10	11-13	14-16	17-19

lated to stroke efficiency, such as swimming speed, amount of kick used, etc., can affect the number of strokes you take; but keeping in mind its limitations, it can be useful. To make your stroke count as meaningful as possible, you should try to swim at a constant pace or tempo each time you apply the test.

During the time you are in the first phase of training, the workouts should consist of a warm-up sufficiently long to loosen you up and leave you ready to concentrate on your stroke. A swim of 100 yards, using your best stroke, a series of one length kicks, either with or without a kickboard, or kicking while holding on to the side of the pool for maybe four 30-second periods, with a 30-second rest between each kicking effort, and two to six one-length swims would give you a good warm-up. The swims you do following your warm-up should be of relatively short distance and separated by plenty of rest so that you are assured of being able to concentrate on your stroke rather than on how tired you are getting.

When you have developed your stroke technique in the stroke you are working on to the point where you have brought your stroke count down at least into the "good" range and you are comfortable with it, being able to swim 100 yards with relative ease, you are ready to begin work on extending your distance capabilities.

Training Phase Two — Developing Your Distance Capabilities

In this phase of your training program, you will be able to measure progress, and set goals much more rapidly than was possible in the stroke development phase just completed. Of course you must always be mindful of using proper technique in this and all subsequent training so as not to lapse into old mistakes as you tire or strive particularly hard to reach your distance or speed goals along the way.

A reasonable goal for you as an advanced swimmer would be to swim continuously for one mile. Greater distances may, of course, be strived for in the setting of your personal goals, but, as a guideline for when you are ready to move on to your next phase of training, a mile is certainly adequate. Once you have swum the mile, you will have developed your capabilities to the point where additional yardage may become more tedius than satisfying. As your own coach, you should set your personal distance goals for each of your basic strokes. It isn't necessary for you to go a mile with each stroke (certainly not butterfly), but you should be able to swim each stroke at a relaxed pace for an adequate distance to indicate its mastery. Goals of a continuous mile of crawl; 400 yards each of elementary backstroke, back crawl, breaststroke, and sidestroke; and 100 yards of butterfly would not be unreasonable. Having accomplished them, you would certainly be justified in having confidence in your ability and readiness to move into more advanced training.

Here again, as in all phases of training, you should precede the major part of your workout with an adequate warm-up. This is particularly true when you are striving to improve past distance or speed.

In approaching your distance goals you should start with your present distance capability and go on from there, adding yardage with each workout, gauging how far you should go each time by how your stroke and physical condition hold up. When you become so tired that your stroke starts to deteriorate, you should stop and not continue to the point of exhaustion. Certainly you could go farther, but your goal is to swim the distance with good stroke technique, and without great discomfort.

Your distance effort for each workout can be followed (after adequate rest allowing you to fully recover) by a series of shorter repeat swims and kicks utilizing strokes other than those used for distance swim. A typical workout, then, might be as follows:

(a) Warm-up: Swim 100 easy; Kick 2 × 50 with 1-minute rest between 50s; Swim 2 × 50 with a 30-second rest between 50s, at distance pace.
(b) Distance effort: Swim continuous crawl 800 yards. (Rest 10 minutes)
(c) Additional: Swim 3 × 100 with a 1-minute rest between 100s (one 100 each of sidestroke, back crawl, and breaststroke)
Kick 6 × 50 with a 30-second rest between 50s (two 50s each of scissors, whip, and back flutter kick)
Swim 4 × 25 with a 1-minute rest between 25s (at a pace faster than distance pace)
(Total distance: 1,800)

The time available for training and the rate at which you want to progress will determine the make-up of your workout as far as what you do in addition to your distance effort for any particular workout. Naturally, your distance and other goals will be realized sooner with more work. Keep in mind that you can't do it all at once. Set up your program so that you approach your goals steadily but at a pace in keeping with your ability and physical condition. You may just want to warm up, swim your distance effort for the day, and get out of the water. With that limited effort it will take longer to reach your distance goal, but, after all, you are only in competition with yourself, and you can set the pace that best suits you and makes swimming enjoyable.

While it will be a temptation to move ahead into speed training before attaining your basic distance goals, it would not be to your best advantage. The training you go through in building up your distance capabilities accomplishes three things. First, as a follow-up to your first phase of training, it enables you to establish your proper stroke techniques through relaxed and paced swimming to a greater extent than if you go too soon into a program aimed at conditioning and speed development. Secondly, the accomplishment of your distance goals build confidence in swimming and will allow you later to pursue speed goals with an assurance of realizing them. Finally, through paced swimming over longer distances you have been gradually improving your physical condition, so that when you do move into more strenuous training, you will have the conditioning background to do it comfortably.

In order to inject variety into your workouts (while concentrating on distance) you can vary your basic stroke from day to day so that your ability in all the strokes you work on progresses uniformly. You might also alternate straight distance swims with a series of shorter distances swum at your distance pace with a short rest interval between. These short distances, when added up, equal or exceed the longest continuous distance you have swum using the stroke. For example, if you managed to swim continuously for 500 yards in your last workout, you might prepare to swim 600 yards by breaking up the 600 the next day in any of the following ways: 2 × 300; 3 × 200; 6 × 100; 12 × 50; or 24 × 25. Your rest interval between each segment should be long enough to allow you to recover sufficiently to continue the succeeding segment at your regular distance pace.

Following are five consecutive sample workouts that might be used by an advanced swimmer who thus far has managed to swim 600 yards crawl and 200 yards each of breaststroke and back crawl:[1]

1. Key to workout terminology and abbreviations:
    Swim........Use both armstroke and kick.
    Kick........ Kick only, without arm pull, either with or without kickboard.
    Pull .... Pull using arms only, supporting legs with a flotation devise held between legs, or over the feet, such as a small inner tube.
    A series of efforts at a particular distance, and with a set rest interval between each effort in the series, is abbreviated as follows:
    > 8 × 50/30-sec. rest ..... Eight times 50 yards with a 30-second rest between each of the eight 50s.
    > 8 × 50/on 1 min...... Eight times 50 yards, beginning each 50 sixty-seconds after the start of the previous effort. Referred to as "going *on the minute*."

    If multiple series are to be swum, the abbreviated notation would be as follows:
    > 4 × 4 × 50/20-sec. rest/on 6 min...... Go 4 sets of 4 × 50 yards with a 20-second rest between each of the four 50s, beginning each new series 6 minutes after the start of the preceding series (going *on the 6 minutes*).

    If the efforts in a series are to be done at a particular pace, the notation would be as follows:
    > Swim 4 × 100/1-min. rest @ 1:10 ..... Swim 4 times 100 yards with 1-minute rest between each of the 100s, and swimming each 100 at a pace of 1-minute and 10 seconds.

(1) Warm-up: Swim 100 breast; Swim 2 × 50 (crawl @ distance pace)/1-min. rest
     Swim 600 crawl (rest 5 minutes)
     Kick 2 × 50/ on 2 min. (whip), 2 × 50/ on 2 min. (back flutter)
     Swim 4 × 50/ 1-min. rest (breast)

(2) Warm-up: Swim 200 (50 each of breast, back, side, and crawl)
     Kick 2 × 50/30-sec. rest (flutter kick)
     Swim 4 × 25/30-sec. rest
     Swim 8 × 100 crawl/ adequate rest between 100s to maintain pace (Rest 5 minutes)
     Kick 8 × 50/30-sec. rest. (Two 50s each of whip, back flutter, scissors, and flutter)

(3) Warm-up: Swim 100 crawl
     Kick 4 × 50/30-sec. rest (vary kick used)
     Swim 4 × 25/30-sec. rest (breast, back, side, crawl)
     Swim 250 yards breaststroke (Rest 5 minutes)
     Kick 4 × 50/ adequate rest to recover (back flutter kick)
     Swim 100 crawl (easy)
     Swim 4 × 25/ adequate rest to fully recover (Back crawl)

(4) Warm-up: Swim 100 (25 each of crawl, side, breast, and back)
               Kick 100 breast (whip)
               Swim 4× 25/15 to 30 sec. rest @ distance pace
      Swim 4 × 200/ adequate rest to maintain pace (crawl) (Rest 10 min.)
      Kick 4 × 50/ adequate rest to recover (breaststroke)
      Swim 8 × 25/15 breaths rest (back crawl)

(5) Warm-up: Swim 200 crawl easy; Kick 8 × 25/30 sec. rest (2 flutter,
               2 whip kick, 4 back flutter); Swim 4 × 25/15 breaths rest
               (alternate breast and back crawl)
      Swim 300 back crawl (Rest until fully recovered)
      Kick 4 × 100/ adequate rest (2 whip kick, 2 flutter)
      Swim 4 × 25/15 breaths rest @ stronger than distance pace

Training Phase Three — Speed and Physical Condition

After you have accomplished your distance goals and have perfected your technique in swimming the strokes you have concentrated on, you can begin working specifically on speed and cardiovascular development. These aspects, of course, have been developing collaterally during Phase Two, but now particular attention will be paid to them as training is planned with speed and physical conditioning goals in mind.

Organization of workouts — Since you are now going to be working with time, it is obvious that a timing devise of some sort is required if you are to more than guess at your progress. Nearly all competitive teams use a large pace clock, approximately three feet in diameter, which can be set at or near poolside so that all swimmers can easily see it as they start and finish each swimming effort. Lacking a pace clock, a large wall clock with a sweep second hand, a waterproof wristwatch, or an instructor or friend with a stopwatch or wristwatch will suffice. You are now ready to set up your orderly workout with your clock playing an integral part.

Using your clock is easy, and it will allow you to plan and swim your workouts in a very orderly fashion. Assume that your pace clock is a large poolside model, with a 60-second face, numbered in 5-second intervals, with large sweep second and minute hands (figure 29). If you are to swim 20 times 50 yards in a 25 yard pool, you could, for instance, begin each effort as the second hand passes "60" on the clock (20 × 50/on 1 min.). If you can swim 50 yards in 35 seconds, you will then have a 25-second rest before starting the succeeding 50 yard swim, etc. To give yourself more rest you can plan to go every 1 1/2 minutes, so that you will alternately start at "60" and "30." In that case, you will get 55 seconds rest between each 50 yard swim if you maintain your 35-second pace. Using this method of starting each effort at a set time allows you to plan your workout precisely to fit into whatever time you may have allotted for your training. For instance, you will be able to finish 20 × 50/on 1 min. in just short of 20 minutes or 20 × 50/on 1 1/2 min., in just over 29 minutes (excluding the rest period following the 20th 50-yard effort).

An alternate way of setting up your series of repeat efforts (e.g., 20 × 50 again), would be to take an exact amount of rest between each effort. So, if you decide to swim 20 × 50 with a 30-second rest between 50s, you would start the first 50 on "60," finishing in 35 seconds and start the second 50 when the second hand reaches "5" on the clock (exactly 30 seconds after the finish of the preceding effort, etc.). Using this method, you will get a full 30-second rest no matter how slow you go, whereas using the first method, as you get slower, your rest interval gets shorter. This latter method, however, is a bit more complicated, and you will have to pay close attention to the clock throughout in order to know how fast you are going and when you are to start the next repeat.

Figure 29—Pace clock.

Using a pace clock in the ways suggested above will allow several swimmers to train at the same time with each knowing just how fast he is swimming. More than one swimmer can train at one time in each lane of the pool very efficiently as long as all swimmers in the same lane are doing the same workout. Thus, with two swimmers in a lane, you could go 20 × 50/on 1 min. by having one swimmer start at "60," and the other at "30," keeping to the right to avoid collisions. Similarly, three swimmers could go in one lane by having one start at "60," the second at "20," and the third at "40." This allows adequate spacing between swimmers, and if they keep to the right within their lane as they swim, they will not be interrupted throughout the series. (Figure 30.)

Variety — You should inject variety into the workouts in your training program from now on by using different strokes from time to time. This will not only keep things interesting, but it will leave you in well-rounded condition, ready for whatever aquatic activity may come along. Using different strokes in your training gives you still another variable you can utilize to add greater variety to your workouts.

Utilizing Training Time — It will generally be the case that you have a set amount of time in which to train. That being so, you can set up an endless

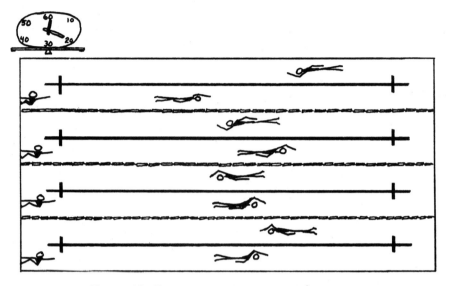

Figure 30—Organization of team interval training.

variety of combinations of swimming, kicking, and pulling efforts separated by varying rest intervals directed toward your goals of speed improvement and enhanced cardiovascular condition, which, by preplanning, will fit into your alloted time.

As you get under way in the speed and physical conditioning training program, you may start with a total workout yardage of as little as 1,000 yards and progress gradually to as much as 3,000 yards in a one-hour period. In the early stages of your conditioning program you should allow yourself plenty of rest between efforts. As you get in better shape through training, you will be able to cut down the rest interval and thus increase daily yardage while still keeping within the one-hour training period. You can also increase the intensity of your one-hour workout by picking up the pace, even though you may not increase the total yardage you are swimming.

Assuming then, that you have one hour in which to train, the following sample workouts illustrate how you might utilize that time period at various stages of your development:

(1) Warm-up: Swim 4 × 50/30-sec. rest (back, breast, side, free),
          Kick 200 (vary kick), Swim 4 × 25/on 1 min.
    Swim 400 (Rest 8 minutes)
    Kick 2 × 100/1-min. rest
    Swim 6 × 50/on 1:30
    Kick 100 easy
    Swim 4 × 25/on 2 min. @ strong pace
    (56 minutes — 1,600 yards)

(2) Warm-up: Swim 200, Kick 4 × 25/30-sec. rest, Swim 4 × 25/30-sec.
          rest

Swim "Locomotive" to 4 and back (1 length hard, 1 easy, 2 hard, 2 easy,
    3 hard, 3 easy, 4 hard, 4 easy, 3 hard, 3 easy, 2 hard, 2 easy, 1 hard)
Kick 2 × 200/ on 6 min. (choice of kick)
Swim 3 × 200/1-min. rest (breast, sidestroke, backstroke)
(Approx. 55 minutes — 2,050 yards)
(3) Warm-up: Swim 100, Kick 100, Swim 4 × 50/30-sec. rest (back, breast,
    sidestroke, freestyle)
Swim 4 × 100/ on 2:30 (all same stroke)
Kick 4 × 100/ on 3:30 (vary kick used)
Swim 4 × 4 × 50/30-sec. rest/2-min. rest between series (one series
    each of breaststroke, back crawl, sidestroke, freestyle)
(55 minutes — 2,000 yards)

Planning your workouts under the interval training system so that you
can finish your work in the time allotted for your training session is easy if
you have an available timing devise, and if your workout is set up ahead of
time. Thus, if you have 45 minutes to train from the time you enter the pool
until you leave it, you could set up the workout as follows:

Warm-up: Swim 100, Kick 100, Swim 2 × 50/1-min. rest   (10 min.)
Swim 10 × 50/ on 1:30   (15 min.)
Kick 4 × 100/ on 3:30   (14 min.)
Swim 8 × 25/ on :45   (6 min.)
(Total yards: 1,400 ....Total time: 45 min.)

Broken-Distance Training — In working to improve speed over a given
distance, a devise widely used in training competitive swimmers is the
"broken-distance swim." For instance, if you were trying to improve your
time for 400 yards, you could break the 400 up into various segments. For
example, you could go 2 × 200, 4 × 100, 8× 50, 16 × 25, or various combinations, such as, 200 plus 100 plus 2 × 50. If the goal is to swim the 400 free
in 4:40, you would try to swim each segment of your "broken 400" at a pace
which if continued for the full distance would give you that time. Therefore,
if you are going to swim 8 × 50, you should try to go each 50 in at least 35
seconds. If going 4 × 100, you would try to hold 1:10 for each 100, etc.

Early in your training, you will want to break your total distance (400
yards, or whatever) into small segments (e.g., 25s or 50s) and give yourself
an adequate set rest period between each segment to allow you to recover
sufficiently to maintain your desired pace. When you are able to hold the
pace throughout, then you can begin decreasing the rest interval and breaking the total distance into larger segments. For example, when you are starting training, you might go 8 × 50/1-min. rest (that is, you take exactly a
1-minute rest between each of the eight 50s). As you find you are able to hold
your pace with that much rest, you will gradually decrease your rest interval
from 1 minute, until you are resting only as long as 5 or 10 seconds between
50s. Similarly, you may start by going in 50-yard segments, and gradually get
to the point where you can go 2 × 200, with less and less rest, holding the
same pace that will give you your 4:40 400. The broken-distance progression
gradually decreases rest and then gradually increases the distance of each
segment. It can make striving for your time goals interesting and challenging.

Below is a progression of broken 400s that might be used by a swimmer striving to ultimately swim a straight 400 yards in 4 minutes and 40 seconds. The rest intervals shown indicate the exact amount of rest he is to take from the time he finishes one segment of his broken 400 until he starts the next. The speed indicated is the pace that must be held in order to swim 400 yards in the time set as a goal (4:40).

8 × 50/1½m @ :35..

8 × 50/1m @ :35..

8 × 50/40s @ :35........4 × 100/2m @ 1:10...

8 × 50/30s @ :35........4 × 100/1:30 @ 1:10...

8 × 50/20s @ :35........4 × 100/1:10 @ 1:10...

8 × 50/10s @ :35........4 × 100/1m @ 1:10........2 × 200/4m @ 2:20

8 × 50/5s @ :35........4 × 100/30s @ 1:10........2 × 200/2m @ 2:20

....4 × 100/20s @ 1:10........2 × 200/1½m @ 2:20

....4 × 100/10s @ 1:10........2 × 200/1m @ 2:20

....2 × 200/30s @ 2:20

Of course you can fill in your times, distances, and rest intervals depending on the time-distance goals you set. The variety that this method allows in your training keeps interest up and gives you something to shoot for each day. You don't have the drudgery of doing the same thing day after day, yet you are closing in on your goals.

It is easy to time yourself for your broken distance swims with a pace clock or a sweep second hand that can be seen easily from the water. The following sample broken 400s show just how it is done.

(1) Swim 8 × 50/1-min. rest between each 50-yard swim. If both the minute and second hands are at "60" on your clock as you start the first 50-yard swim, and if you take exactly a 1-minute rest between 50s, you will subtract 7 minutes (the total of the 7 rest intervals) from your finish time on the clock. You will then have your equivalent 400 time. If you did manage to hold a 35-second pace throughout, your finish time on the clock will actually be exactly 11:40. From that time you subtract your 7 minutes of rest to arrive at your equivalent 400 time of 4:40.

(2) Swim 4 × 100/30 seconds rest between each 100-yard swim. Starting again on "60," you would subtract 1 minute and 30 seconds (the total of the 3 rest intervals) from your total elapsed time on the clock to arrive at your equivalent 400-yard time.

You can avoid having to subtract at the end by figuring out your total rest interval ahead of time and starting that much time ahead of "60." Thus, in our first example (8 × 50/1-min. rest), you would start the minute hand at "53" and the second hand at "60." You then swim your 8 × 50 yards taking the prescribed rest, and if you have held a 35-second pace throughout, the time on the clock will be 4:40 as you finish your 8th 50-yard swim. Similarly, you would start 1 minute and 30 seconds early if you were doing your broken 400 as designated in the second example above (4 × 100/30 seconds rest).

Your training can be made even more interesting and challenging if you simultaneously set goals at different distances and in more than one stroke. You could, for instance, set goals for 100, 200, and 400 crawl, along with 100 breaststroke and 100 backstroke. In your weekly workout plan, you could concentrate on your 400 crawl on Monday, 100 back on Tuesday, 200 crawl on Wednesday, 100 breaststroke on Thursday, and 100 crawl on Friday. Your training on each will naturally improve performance on the others, but because the emphasis is different, your interest will be kept at a high level.

Getting Ready For Your Optimum Performance — Swimmers who conscientiously follow a training program for a period of time find their overall speed improving with their physical condition, even though they are working hard each day without giving themselves a real chance to rest up. However, in order to fully realize the effect of a prolonged training program, the swimmer must give himself a chance to rest and to sharpen his reactions through what is known in competitive swimming as a "tapering-and-peaking" period. What is done during this period, as the phrases indicate, is to "taper," or cut down, the amount of work being done in order to bring the swimmer into "peak" condition for a top effort, by placing more emphasis on pure speed, as opposed to conditioning, efforts. This allows the swimmer's body to come up to full strength and preparedness for an all-out effort. The duration of the tapering-and-peaking period might be as long as three weeks for a competitive swimmer who has been training heavily for up to three months. During the first week of the taper, the swimmer's training yardage would gradually drop from a mid-season average of perhaps 10,000 yards to 4,000 yards, including a long warm-up and several high-quality, long-rest efforts. During the second week, the yardage would drop even further as coach and swimmer concentrate on pace, speed, and technique. The final week before a championship competition would likely find the swimmer going less than 2,000 yards with a long warm-up, a very limited number of high quality efforts swum at race pace, and some very short efforts designed to sharpen his starting and turning techniques.

Following a prolonged training period, you might consider tapering and peaking yourself for as long as a two-week period to see what times you can achieve when fully rested. Of course, if you are not really extending yourself in your training prior to the peaking period, you can't expect much of an improvement in your times after resting since you probably were not very tired to begin with.

Pulse Rate — Certainly your overall physical condition will be improving greatly as you take part in distance and speed training, as achievement of your goals in these areas will clearly show. In addition to these measures of progress, you can, to a certain extent, use your pulse rate and the changes it undergoes as you train to further monitor your improving physical condition. During physical exertion, normal resting pulse rate (e.g., 70 beats per minute) will increase according to the intensity and duration of the exertion. During a series of repeat swims (e.g., 8 $\times$ 50/10-second rest), done at a strong pace, your pulse rate will increase greatly. It is not uncommon for competitive swimmers during training to develop pulse rates well in excess of 160 beats per minute during and immediately following a hard series of swims.

Have you practiced taking your pulse count immediately following a swimming effort? Have you charted your recovery rate to compare it with future efforts?

One measure frequently used today as an indicator of a swimmer's physical condition is his "recovery rate"—that is, the rate at which his pulse count returns toward normal during a rest following a given effort. To test yourself, you should select a set swimming effort (e.g., 200 yards crawl, or 4 × 50 with a 20-second rest between 50s, swim at a strong pace) which you will use each time you test yourself. Immediately after finishing the swim or series of swims, take your pulse for a 10-second period using the carotid artery found below your chin and just to the side of your esophagus. You will discover that it takes a bit of practice to find your pulse rapidly and to count it just after a swimming effort. One minute after you finish your swim take your pulse again, and then a third time, one minute later. To get the full pulse count for each segment of your recovery time, multiply each 10-second count by 6. You might end up with rates of 150, 125, and 110, respectively. Using these counts as the base, repeat the test once a week during the training period and chart the results. As your physical condition improves, your pulse rate will return to its resting count more rapidly. You can similarly check your pulse immediately following a given effort (e.g., 100 yards crawl @ 1:10) and chart your rate each week. As your stroke efficiency and/or physical condition improves, the final pulse should be lower, indicating a decreasing effort necessary on your part to perform the set swim. This decreased effort will be the result of an improved stroke efficiency, improved physical condition, or a combination of the two. Whatever the cause, you will know you are improving.

For each of these tests, you should use as your "set effort" a distance or set of repeat swims that will tax you sufficiently to have a meaningful change of pulse rate. In other words, you won't be able to see much improvement when you go a set of 4 × 50 yards with a set rest interval at 40 seconds for each 50 if you can go the same set with a fairly hard effort at 30 seconds for each 50.

Rules of Swimming 5

Although advanced swimming as such is unemcumbered by rules other than the common sense ones relating to safety, cleanliness, and good manners, as the advanced swimmer branches out into the various aquatic activities and as his swimming ability opens up to him such skills as synchronized swimming, water polo, skin and scuba diving, and competitive swimming, he will find many written and unwritten rules defining his actions in these areas. Although for the most part the rules controlling these specialized activities are not within the scope of this book, they can be readily found in the publications specifically dedicated to them which are suggested for reading in the Selected References section of this book, following Chapter 8. However, since all advanced swimmers utilize the strokes and many of the techniques of competitive swimming, it will be useful to look at the rules specifically defining and limiting them. The following rules defining competitive swimming strokes are taken from the Official Collegiate—Scholastic Swimming Guide.[1] To the extent that the rules are quoted below, they are essentially uniform throughout the world of swimming.

Freestyle — a. In a freestyle event, any style or combination of styles may be used.
    b. A hand touch is not required at the turn; it is sufficient if any part of the body touches the end of the pool on each turn.

Breaststroke — a. The breaststroke must be swum on the surface. Following the take-off and each turn, one arm-pull and one leg-kick may be taken underwater, but some portion of the contestant's head must break the surface of the water before another stroke is started. Except for this provision, some portion of the contestant's head must be higher than the normal, flat surface of the water at all times.
    b. Both hands must be pushed forward simultaneously on or under the surface of the water and brought backward simultaneously.
    c. The body must be kept perfectly on the breast, with both shoulders in a horizontal plane.
    d. The feet shall be drawn up with the knees bent and apart. The movement shall be continued with a rounded outward sweep of the feet bringing the legs together. Up and down movements of the legs in the vertical plane are prohibited. All movements of the legs and feet must be simultaneous, and in the same horizontal plane. A contestant may not introduce a sidestroke movement,

---

1. *Official Collegiate - - - Scholastic Swimming Guide.* College Athletics Publishing Service, 349 East Thomas Road, Phoenix, Arizona (Annual).

or use the top of the instep of one or both feet in the propulsive part of the breaststroke kick.

Butterfly — a. Both arms must be brought forward together over the water and brought backward simultaneously.

b. The body must be kept perfectly on the breast, and both shoulders in the horizontal plane.

c. All up and down movements of both legs and feet must be simultaneous and may not be of an alternating nature.

d. When a contestant is in the underwater position after the start, when turning, or during the race, he is allowed to make one or more kicks.

e. A contestant may not introduce a scissor or breaststroke kicking movement.

Backstroke — a. The contestant shall push off on his back and continue swimming on his back throughout the race.

b. A hand touch is required at each turn and the contestant's hips may not turn over beyond the vertical before his foremost hand has touched the end of the pool.

Note: Portions of the rules governing breaststroke and butterfly, particularly regarding turns, are omitted.

Individual Medley — The contestant shall swim the prescribed distance as follows: the first one-fourth, butterfly; the second one-fourth, backstroke; the third one-fourth, breaststroke, and the last one-fourth, freestyle. In the individual medley, the term "freestyle" designates any style other than butterfly, backstroke or breaststroke.

Relays — The lead-off man starts with the pistol shot. Each succeeding teammate assumes the forward starting position with both feet in contact with the starting mark in time to take off the instance the previous swimmer finishes his leg of the race. He may be in motion, but must still be in contact with the front edge of the starting block when the preceding swimmer finishes.

Unwritten Laws and Hints
for Safety and Comfort
in the Water

6

Ordinary rules of pool safety and conduct need not be reiterated here. The advanced swimmer is well acquainted with them, whether posted or not, since common sense and courtesy provide the basis upon which such rules are made. There are a number of unwritten laws, however, which apply particularly to the advanced swimmer as his expanding capabilities enable him to take advantage of swimming's many opportunities.

Know Your Limitations — Perhaps the most important of swimming's unwritten laws is the caution that you *know your limitations* and act accordingly. Impetuous action without consideration of capabilities can have tragic consequences. Striking off to swim across a lake or river, going out into a surf beyond your ability, and diving from a too-high point are examples of impulsive actions that can lead to trouble. As you seek to expand your abilities beyond present limitations, you should have competent instruction and assistance.

Respect Moving Water — In addition to knowing and abiding by your limitations, you should have proper respect for the force of moving water, whether it be the ocean with its powerful surf, tides, and currents, or rivers and streams, whose currents can make light of your best swimming efforts. The force of a breaking wave or rushing water is formidable, and learning to handle the surf and surge of the ocean takes time, caution, and the help of an accomplished ocean swimmer. You must accept the ocean on its own terms.

Follow the Buddy System — Although mentioned in other chapters, the universal unwritten law of swimming—that you adhere to the "buddy system," can well be repeated here. With a buddy you always have someone who knows where you are, what you are doing, and who can help or summon help when you need it. Even in a crowded pool situation with lifeguards present, this caution is vital. It is impossible for the lifeguard to keep everyone in view all the time. Buddies can always be aware of what the other is doing. When you become involved in lake, river, or ocean swimming, it is all the more important that you don't swim alone. Unforeseen things, such as cramps, fatigue, illness, or injury can and do happen to the best swimmers, and a buddy can help when the unexpected arises.

Use a Reaching Assist — Another law which has been mentioned before must be restated; it is the one that is a guiding principle of lifesaving. You should *never make a swimming rescue in deep water except as a last resort,* and maybe not even then. You should be familiar with all possible "reaching assists." Prepare yourself ahead of time in all swimming situations by knowing what is available for use in reaching a drowning victim—ring bouys, poles, ropes, boats, surf boards, etc. If you are not a fully-trained lifeguard, you are very likely to find yourself in trouble when you go into the water to rescue a victim who is panicky and uncontrollable. Your well-meaning but impulsive effort could well end in double tragedy. There is almost always *something* that can be extended to the victim to hold on to, and with which you can pull him to the side or to shore.

Don't Scuba Dive Without Proper Training — Another caution that you might not otherwise consider as you become a strong swimmer and desire to delve into all of swimming's exciting aspects is that you not use scuba gear without first becoming properly certified by taking a full course of instruction in its use. A full course of instruction generally will run thirty or more hours—there *is* that much to learn. While equipment may be available which seems easy to use, (mechanically, it is), you can gravely injure yourself by breathing compressed air underwater without knowing the basic physics and physiology involved and without observing the proper procedures that must be followed in order to assure safe diving. The unwritten law for scuba-diving-shop operators requires them to ask for proof of your certification before selling you either scuba equipment or air for your scuba tanks. However, not all dive-shop operators adhere to this policy; so it is up to you to safeguard yourself by first getting certified. You can then enjoy the wonders of scuba diving.

Don't Panic — A final unwritten law of swimming is *don't panic.* If kept in mind when the occasion arises, it may well save your life. It may be difficult to keep cool as the feeling of fear comes on you in a difficult swimming situation, but you must do so. Panic causes us to do things that we would never try to do otherwise and to forget to do the elementary things that could save us. Panic also causes a flow of adrenaline that quickly saps strength when it is most needed. It's the panic-striken man who, rather than reaching with a branch or rope or realizing the hopelessness of the situation, jumps into the river to save a child and drowns with him. It is the panic-stricken person who tries to buck a riptide to the point of exhaustion rather than riding it out. And it's sad, but true, that most scuba divers who drown while diving in cold water with wet suits on and lead weight belts to counteract the bouyancy of the wet suit, drown with the weight belt still on, when all they had to do was release it to float quickly to the surface by the great bouyancy of the wet suit. As an advanced swimmer, you can keep yourself afloat for a long period of time if you have to. So keep your wits about you in any situation. It's the sign of a true waterman.

Handling Swimming's Physical Hazards and Discomforts

In addition to the various cautions given above and elsewhere throughout this book directed to the avoidance of swimming's more serious hazards are the following hints on how to prevent or treat some of swimming's more frequent but less serious discomforts.

Cold — Swimming is most comfortable when the water temperature is in the 75- to 80-degree range. Cold water should be entered with consideration for your vital processes. It may be more spectacular to run and dive into the water after baking in the sun for a while, but it will be much less shock to your system if you do it by degrees. The development of the wet suit, made of foam neoprene and available in various thicknesses from 1/8 to 1/2 inch thick has made swimming, surfing, and particularly skin and scuba diving comfortably possible, even in water colder than 50 degrees.

Cramp — The most common muscle cramps for swimmers are those oc-curing in the legs as a consequence of fatigue brought on by hard exercise or cold. When a muscle cramps, it contracts tightly, and to relieve the condition you must stretch the muscle out. Thus, to relieve a cramp in the calf straighten your leg, and with the knee extended flex your ankle, thereby forcing the heel down and toes up, to stretch the calf muscle. When you get into shallow water or on the deck, you should step backward on the cramped leg, forcing the heel down to the ground thereby stretching the calf muscle and relieving the cramp. Cramps in the upper leg are more difficult to re-lieve, but the stretching process is the way to relief.

Ear Infection — Ear infection ("swimmer's ear") is a common problem for those who swim in lowland lakes, rivers, and streams, and, to an extent, for swimmer's in general. Because of the impurity of most untreated waters in which people swim, bacteria are likely to thrive in a swimmer's ear if he doesn't thoroughly dry it out after swimming. Placing a couple of drops of 50-70% alcohol in each ear and allowing it to run out will promote rapid dry-ing and is quite successful in preventing "swimmer's ear."

Ear Pain Caused By Pressure — The cause and prevention of ear pain as a swimmer descends from the surface is thoroughly discussed in the Under-water Swimming section of Chapter 2.

Eye Irritation — Eye irritation caused by a chemical imbalance in the swimming pool water can only be successfully avoided by wearing goggles. Competitive swimmers who swim up to several hours a day frequently wear goggles during training periods. Commercial eye-drop preparations are available which relieve eye irritation following swimming; they do so with varying degrees of success.

Knee Pain — With the development of the whip kick and its emphasis on outward rotation of the leg and the sweeping of the feet down and around outside the knees during the power phase of the kick, some amount of pain and damage in the knee joint have occasionally resulted. Swimmers using the whip kick should work into it gradually over a period of weeks and should be careful to warm up the kick gradually before kicking full strength on any particular day as well. The muscles around the knee joint can be strengthened by doing knee extension exercises and by utilizing a gradually increasing resistance.

Shallow Water Blackout — See the Underwater Swimming section of Chapter 2 for a full discussion of this very real swimming hazard which may result from the use of hyperventilation to extend breath-holding capabilities.

7 Language and Lore of Advanced Swimming

As with any specialized field, swimming has a great many terms that are either peculiar to the sport or have different meanings when used in a swimming context. These and several other terms that will be encountered by the advanced swimmer are defined below. Many of the following terms are the subject of in-depth discussion in the text of this book; in these instances, chapter references are given in parenthesis.

Back Crawl — The swimming stroke commonly used by competitive swimmers in backstroke competition. The stroke is done on the back, and it utilizes the alternating arm stroke of the crawl with over-the-water recovery and an alternating up and down flutter kick (2).

Bent Arm Stroke — Refers to the bent position of the arm *midway* through the power phase of a swimming armstroke to effect proper and more efficient application of force through the power phase as opposed to keeping the elbow fully extended through the power phase of any swimming stroke (2).

Breaststroke — An internationally popular stroke upon which primary emphasis is placed at the beginning level in many European countries. Breaststroke is one of the basic competitive strokes; it is done in a prone position utilizing a simultaneous double arm with an under-the-water recovery, alternating with a simultaneous and symmetrical leg kick in which the feet are recovered toward the buttocks with knees bent, and then swept around to full extension, providing a backward thrust (2, 5).

Broken-Distance Swim — A term used in swim training to designate the segmenting of a given distance (e.g., 400 yards) into a series of shorter efforts (e.g., 8 × 50 yards) with a set short interval of rest (e.g., 20 seconds) taken between each effort. Thus, 8 × 50 yards with a 20-second rest between 50s is a "broken 400" (4).

Buddy System — The unwritten rule of all swimming that requires you to swim with a buddy rather than alone so that in times of distress your buddy will be there to assist you.

Butterfly — A competitive swimming stroke done in a prone position utilizing a simultaneous double-arm stroke with an over-the-water recovery, and the simultaneous, up-and-down kick known as the "dolphin" kick (2, 5).

Cardiovascular Conditioning — Physical training, such as swimming, for the purpose of developing and improving the efficiency of the body's oxygen transport and distribution system (4).

Catch — The point just prior to the power phase of a swimming stroke where the swimmer's hand starts to press downward and he can feel the pressure of the water on it as he "catches" hold in preparation for the pull.

Certified Scuba Diver — A person who has been certified by a recognized certifying agency (N.A.U.I., Y.M.C.A., Los Angeles County, etc.), as having satisfactorily completed a course of lessons in scuba diving.

Clearing Your Ears — Equalizing the pressure in the middle ear to that of the surrounding water as a swimmer descends from the surface (thus avoiding pain and possible rupture of the eardrum) by enabling air to pass from the breathing passageways through the eustachion tube to the middle ear (1).

Cramp — The involuntary contraction of a muscle for a prolonged time due primarily to fatigue (6).

Crawl — A swimming stroke swum in a prone position utilizing an alternating front-to-back arm stroke with an over-the-water recovery and an alternating up-and-down leg kick (the flutter kick). The number of kicks varies from one to six for each complete arm cycle (2).

Drownproofing — A method of sustaining oneself in deep water for prolonged periods of time with a minimum of effort; developed by the late Professor Fred R. Lanoue of the Georgia Institute of Technology. Drownproofing utilizes a headdown "jellyfish"-type floating position in combination with a rhythmically executed scissors kick and a relaxed double-arm push downward as the head is raised for a breath every 3 to 10 seconds.

Elementary Backstroke — An excellent resting stroke done on the back and utilizing an arm stroke wherein the hands are recovered underwater along the sides of the body to above the waist, then fully extended out to the sides for a sweeping power stroke down to the legs. The kick done simultaneously with the arm stroke is the "whip kick" used in breaststroke swimming. Following the simultaneous pull and kick, the swimmer should glide for from 2 to 5 seconds before recovering his arms and legs for the next stroke.

Eustachion Tube — The tube connecting the middle ear with the breathing passageway through which air passes to maintain an equilibrium of pressure between the middle and outer ear.

"Finish" of a Stroke — The final application of force during the power phase of a swimming stroke. The last 1/3 of the power phase of a stroke. Often ignored by beginners, this element of the arm stroke is emphasized by competitive swimmers.

Flip Turn — The racing turn used by competitive swimmers in the crawl and back crawl strokes. In the crawl, or "freestyle" flip turn, the swimmer does a somersault with a one-quarter twist so that he is on his side as he pushes off from the wall. In the back-flip turn the swimmer actually pivots on his back as his legs come around through the air to the wall for the push off (3).

Flutter Kick — An alternating up-and-down kicking action of the legs and feet with legs fully extended along the surface of the water, the knees bending slightly only at the initiation of the downward kick, when done in a prone position or at the initiation of the upward kick when swimming on the back (2).

Freestyle — Actually defined in competitive swimming as, ". . . any style or combination of styles . . . ," "freestyle" is the name commonly applied to crawl stroke.

Grab Start — A racing start in which the swimmer leans over and holds on with his hands to the leading edge of the starting block at the starter's command to take your mark. On the signal to go, he pushes against the block with his hands to quickly get his body moving forward in preparation for his dive (3).

Hyperventilation — Rapid and deep in-and-out breathing, usually in an effort to extend breath-holding capabilities. Effect is to "wash out" CO_2 from the circulation system, prolonging the time a person can hold his breath without feeling the urge to breath, which is triggered by CO_2 buildup. Dangerous because oxygen depletion can cause one to black out before realization of the *need* to breath (2).

Interval Training — A training technique utilizing series of repeated efforts done at a strong pace and separated by specified rest intervals (4).

Layout — A designation of body position used in competitive diving wherein the body is held straight during execution of the dive without bending at the hips or knees.

N.A.U.I. — National Association of Underwater Instructors. A nationally recognized organization devoted to the training of skin and scuba divers and instructors.

Olympic-Size Pool — A designation very commonly misused to describe the dimensions of a swimming pool. An "Olympic-size" pool is actually 50 meters in length, and a minimum of 20 meters in width.

Overdistance Training — Training by swimming distances longer than the length of the race being trained for.

Pace — The rate at which a swimmer swims, generally controlled so as to expend his energy evenly throughout his race.

Pace Clock — A large clock with a sweep second hand placed so as to be easily visible from the pool; used extensively in swimming training, particularly under the interval training method.

Pike — A designation of body position used in competitive diving wherein the diver's body is bent at the hips with knees kept fully extended, as in the "jack-knife" dive.

Pull — (1) As a component of a swimming stroke, "pull" refers to the power phase of the arm stroke. (2) As it is used in swimming training, "pull" refers to swimming using the arms only. While pulling (in this context), the feet and legs should be supported by some flotation device so that the body remains in its normal swimming position, generally horizontal to the surface of the water rather than assuming an unnatural angle.

Recovery — (1) The phase of a swimming arm stroke or kick in which the arms or legs are brought back from the "finish" of the power phase to the point where the power phase begins. (2) When used in connection with pulse rate, "recovery" refers to the reduction in pulse rate over a period of time following a swimming effort as the pulse gradually returns to its "resting" rate (4).

> **Do you know a "rip-tide" from an "undertow"? Do you know how far a "rip-tide" is likely to carry you from shore? Do you know how to get out of a "rip-tide"? How?**

Rescue Breathing — The method of artificial respiration effected by mouth-to-mouth exchange of air between a rescuer and a nonbreathing victim. By far the most efficient nonmechanical means of resuscitation yet devised (3).

Rip-tide — A current of water moving away from the shoreline caused by a concentration of water returning to the sea after being cast on a beach by wave action (3).

Scuba — A word made up of the first letters of the words in the phrase "self-contained underwater breathing apparatus" and referring to that branch of underwater activity in which the swimmer utilizes scuba gear.

Series — A set number of repeated swims at a given distance with a given rest interval as would be performed while training under the interval-training method.

Shaving Down — The act by competitive swimmers of shaving exposed body hair prior to an important race in an attempt to reduce drag as the body goes through the water.

Snorkle — A short, hollow tube through which a swimmer can breath while swimming face down in the water; allows uninterrupted viewing of the underwater scene.

Swimmer's Ear — A term commonly used in referring to ear infection caused by failure to properly dry the outer ear following swimming and the consequent growth of infectious bacteria therein (6).

Tapering — Gradually reducing the amount of yardage a swimmer is swimming in training following an extended training period and as a part of the final preparation for an important meet or race (4).

Tuck — A designation of body position used in competitive diving wherein the diver's knees are flexed and brought to his chest; in this very compact position he can achieve maximum spin for difficult somersault dives.

Warm-up — A period of light exercise or swimming prior to the beginning of more intense training or competition to allow the body and its circulation system to begin operating at a level consistant with the demands that will be placed on it.

Whip Kick — The most efficient evolution of the breaststroke kick widely used by competitive swimmers, it features a simultaneous and symmetrical recovery of the feet toward the buttocks, followed by a rounded outward sweep of the feet bringing the legs together. During the recovery and power phase of the kick, the knees remain relatively close together so that during their outward sweep the feet are outside the knees (2).

8 Where Do You Go from Here?

From here you go on to a fuller, more enjoyable life than was possible for you without the skills you have now acquired. A whole new dimension of health, enjoyment, competition, and inquiry is opened to you, one that is not available to the beginning, or nonswimmer. The challenge of skin and scuba diving, of life saving, of teaching, of ocean swimming, of competition, of further extending your capabilities, and more can now be taken up by you as you use your swimming abilities to enrich your life experience.

You can find information on all these activities by contacting appropriate groups generally found within your community. Certainly the local chapter of the American Red Cross will advise you regarding lifesaving and water safety instructor courses. For information on competitive aquatics in your area, contact your local swim school, high school, college, swim club, recreation center, Y.M.C.A., or office of the Amateur Athletic Union. If there are no others in your community, start your own swimming, water polo, or synchronized swimming team. You might be amazed at the interest and enthusiasm that you can generate in setting up a men's or women's water team at your Y.M.C.A., recreation center, school, or club. A great Olympic sport, water polo, is very popular in the high schools and colleges of California (a state which has supplied the great majority of our national team players) and is one of the fastest growing sports throughout the country. Another swimming activity that is attracting lots of interest is senior age-group swimming. With the recognition of our need to exercise and of our natural inclination to test ourselves against others, senior age-group swimming is a natural outgrowth. This low-pressure program will give you goals to strive for and great added incentive to train as you swim to a healthier life.

Information as to where you can find proper instruction in skin and scuba diving can be gotten from your local Y.M.C.A. or by writing to the National Association of Underwater Instructors, an internationally recognized agency for the certification of skin and scuba divers and instructors, at 22809 Barton Road, Grand Terrace, California, 92324. With the opportunities for relatively inexpensive travel to the multitude of locations offering beautiful diving that are available to you, you can't afford to pass up this aspect of swimming which has so much excitement and beauty to offer.

To find places and time to train, join your local Y.M.C.A., recreation center, or swim club and work with the aquatics director or coach to have certain times set aside for those interested in developing their swimming capabilities. Using the time available, develop your own training program with the help of the suggestions in Chapter 4 and go to it.

You've now stepped "through the looking glass," and the Wonderful World of Water Sports lies before you. Enjoy, enjoy, enjoy!!!

Selected References

Swimming and Diving — Advanced through Competitive

American National Red Cross. *Swimming and Water Safety.* Washington, D. C.: American National Red Cross, 1968.

Armbruster, David A., Sr.; Allen, Robert H.; and Billingsley, Hobert Sherwood. *Swimming and Diving.* 5th ed. St. Louis: C. V. Mosby Co., 1968.

Clark, Steve. *Competitive Swimming As I See It.* North Hollywood, California: Swimming World Books, 1967.

Counsilman, James E. *The Science of Swimming.* Englewood Cliffs, N. J.: Prentice-Hall, Inc., 1968.

Vickers, Betty J., and Vincent, William J. *Swimming.* Dubuque, Iowa: Wm. C. Brown Company Publishers, 1971.

Guides and Periodical Publications:

Official A.A.U. Swimming Handbook. The Amateur Athletic Union. 233 Broadway, New York, N.Y. (Annual).

Official Collegiate — Scholastic Swimming Guide. College Athletics Publishing Service, 349 East Thomas Road, Phoenix, Arizona, 85012 (Annual).

Swimming World Magazine. Swimming World. 12618 Killion, North Hollywood, California, 91607 (Monthly).

Life Saving

American National Red Cross. *Life Saving and Water Safety,* 2nd ed. Philadelphia: P. Blakiston's Sons & Co., 1937.

Skin and Scuba Diving

Conference for National Cooperation in Aquatics. *The Science of Skin and Scuba Diving.* Rev. ed. New York: Association Press, 196.

Navy Department. *U. S. Navy Diving Manual.* Washington, D. C.: U. S. Government Printing Office, 1968.

Tillman, Albert A. *Skin and Scuba Diving.* Dubuque, Iowa: Wm. C. Brown Company Publishers, 1966.

Water Polo

Antilla, William K. *Water Polo Drills and Playing Hints.* Palo Alto, California: National Press, 1964.

Lambert, Arthur F., and Gaughran, Robert K. *The Technique of Water Polo.* North Hollywood, California: Swimming World Books, 1969.

N.C.A.A. — *Official Water Polo Rules.* College Athletics Publishing Service, 349 East Thomas Road, Phoenix, Arizona 85012 (Annual).